guide

Chesnire

WALKS

Compiled by
Brian Conduit

008

JARROLD
publishing

Acknowledgements
My thanks for the valuable advice and numerous useful
leaflets that I obtained from the local authorities and the
various tourist information centres throughout the area.

Text: Brian Conduit
Photography: Brian Conduit
Editor: Crawford Gillan
Designer: Doug Whitworth

Series Consultant: Brian Conduit

Jarrold Publishing   ISBN 0-7117-2415-6

First published 2003
by Jarrold Publishing

Printed in Belgium
by Proost NV, Turnhout. 1/03

Jarrold Publishing
Pathfinder Guides, Whitefriars, Norwich NR3 1TR
E-mail: info@totalwalking.co.uk
www.totalwalking.co.uk

Front cover: Great Budworth
Previous page: Marbury Village

Contents

Short, easy walks

Walks of modest length, likely to involve some modest uphill walking

More challenging walks which may be longer and/or over more rugged terrain, often with some stiff climbs

MANCHESTER
SALFORD
STOCKPORT
STOKE-ON-TRENT
NEWCASTLE-UNDER-LYME
MACCLESFIELD
CONGLETON
KNUTSFORD
WILMSLOW
ALDERLEY EDGE
CHEADLE
GATLEY
CHEADLE HULME
BRAMHALL
HAZEL GROVE
MARPLE
NEW MILLS
BOLLINGTON
ALTRINCHAM
HALE
SALE
STRETFORD
URMSTON
IRLAM
ECCLES
SWINTON
PENDLEBURY
PRESTWICH
WHITEFIELD
RADCLIFFE
MIDDLETON
CHADDERTON
OLDHAM
ROYTON
SHAW
HEYWOOD
FAILSWORTH
DROYLSDEN
DENTON
HYDE
ROMILEY
DUKINFIELD
STALYBRIDGE
ASHTON-UNDER-LYNE
MOSSLEY
FARNWORTH
KEARSLEY
WALKDEN
ATHERTON
TYLDESLEY
HINDLEY
LEIGH
WORSLEY
LYMM
NORTHWICH
WINSFORD
MIDDLEWICH
SANDBACH
CREWE
ALSAGER
KIDSGROVE
BIDDULPH
LEEK
NANTWICH
MARKET DRAYTON
STONE
Manchester International Airport
Holmes Chapel
Goostrey
Poynton
Handforth
Partington
Warrington
Cheadle
Blythe Bridge
Barlaston
Audlem
Madeley
Keele
Shavington
Haslington
Elworth
Davenham
Hartford
Plumley
Mobberley
Prestbury
Tytherington
Biddulph Moor
Endon
Brown Edge
Kingsley
Werrington
Eccleshall
M6
M60
M56
M62
M61
M66
M67
M602
A34
A50
A523
A54
A53
A500
A51
A556
A537
A536
A534
A52
A520
A5020

Walk	Page	Start	Nat. Grid Reference	Distance	Time
Above Helsby and Frodsham	70	Helsby Hill	SJ487473	7 miles (11.2km)	3 ½ hrs
Around Kelsall	22	Gresty's Waste car park	SJ796654	5 miles (8km)	2 ½ hrs
Astbury Mere and village	24	Astbury Mere Country Park	SJ540686	5 ½ miles (8.9km)	2 ½ hrs
Audlem and the Shropshire Union Canal	34	Audlem	SJ758608	6 miles (9.7km)	3 hrs
Barthomley, Englesea-brook and Weston	67	Barthomley	SJ767525	8 miles (12.9km)	4 hrs
Beeston Castle and the Shropshire Union Canal	48	Beeston Castle	SJ541591	6 ½ miles (10.5km)	3 ½ hrs
Bollington and Nab Head	18	Bollington	SJ405664	3 ½ miles (5.6km)	2 hrs
Bulkeley Hill and Raw Head	80	Higher Burwardsley	SJ857574	6 miles (9.7km)	3 hrs
Caldy Hill, Thurstaston and the Wirral Way	52	Thurstaston	SJ6527657	7 miles (11.3km)	3 ½ hrs
Chester and the River Dee	26	Chester	SJ846626	5 miles (8km)	2 ½ hrs
Dane Valley	20	Brereton Heath Country Park	SJ931781	5 miles (8km)	2 ½ hrs
Delamere Forest	32	Linmere	SJ660436	6 miles (9.7km)	3 hrs
Disley and Lyme Park	42	Disley	SJ752888	6 ½ miles (10.5km)	3 hrs
Dunham Park and the Bridgewater Canal	45	Oldfield Brow	SJ973846	6 ½ miles (10.5km)	3 hrs
Farndon and Churton	39	Farndon	SJ413545	6 ½ miles (10.5km)	3 hrs
Gawsworth Hall and North Rode	36	Gawsworth	SJ887695	6 ½ miles (10.5km)	3 hrs
Hale and the Mersey estuary	16	Hale	SJ469823	5 miles (8km)	2 ½ hrs
Little Budworth Country Park	12	Little Budworth Country Park	SJ590654	4 miles (6.4km)	2 hrs
Malpas	73	Malpas	SJ49174925	9 miles (14.5km)	4 ½ hrs
Mow Cop and Little Moreton Hall	77	Mow Cop and Little Moreton Hall	SJ523565	8 ½ miles (13.7km)	4 hrs
Sandbach	29	Sandbach	SJ550704	6 miles (9.7km)	3 hrs
Shutlingsloe	83	Trentabank car park	SJ961712	6 ½ miles (10.5km)	3 ½ hrs
Tegg's Nose and Macclesfield Forest	86	Tegg's Nose Country Park	SJ950733	8 ½ miles (13.7km)	4 ½ hrs
Timbersbrook and The Cloud	64	Timbersbrook	SJ895627	6 miles (9.7km)	3 hrs
Trent and Mersey Canal and Great Budworth	55	Marbury Country Park	SJ238835	7 miles (11.3km)	3 ½ hrs
Wirral Way, Parkgate and the Dee estuary	61	Hadlow Road Station	SJ332774	8 miles (12.9km)	4 hrs
Wirswall Hill and Big Mere	14	Marbury	SJ562457	3 ½ miles (5.6km)	2 hrs
Wybunbury	58	Wybunbury	SJ700499	7 ½ miles (12.1km)	3 ½ hrs

Comments

There are fine views across the Mersey estuary but also some steep ascents and descents across the wooded cliffs that mark the northern end of the sandstone ridge.

There are attractive wooded stretches on the edge of Delamere Forest and fine views across Cheshire to the hills of North Wales.

The walk starts by a mere and includes a stretch of canal, field paths and an attractive village with an imposing church.

This flat walk, mostly across fields and along a canal towpath, provides open and extensive views.

The walk passes through three villages and there are fine views over the surrounding undulating countryside. A warning for the less agile – there are more than 50 stiles.

The wooded sandstone ridge, crowned by both medieval Beeston Castle and the adjacent 19th-century Peckforton Castle, is the dominant landscape feature of this walk.

The short and relatively easy climb to the summit of Nab Head rewards you with grand and extensive views. Shorter version of walk 2½ miles (4km)

This fine scenic walk, quite steep in places, takes you through beautiful woodland to the highest point on the sandstone ridge.

There is superb woodland and heathland and a modest climb rewards you with fine views over both the Dee and Mersey estuaries.

Attractive riverside meadows beside the Dee, coupled with Chester's numerous historic sites, makes for an absorbing walk.

There are fine views over the Dane valley, an attractive village and, in spring, the chance to see a superb display of daffodils.

An undemanding and highly enjoyable walk through some of the finest remaining parts of Delamere Forest.

The contrasting views take in both Greater Manchester and the moorlands of the Peak District and there is a memorable stretch through Lyme Park, passing in front of the hall.

The walk makes use of both a disused railway track and a canal towpath and the highlight is a walk through Dunham Park, with fine views of the great house.

The opening stretch is mainly across fields between Farndon and Churton; the return leg is beside the River Dee.

Half-timbered Gawsworth Hall makes a picturesque focal point for this walk through a typical Cheshire landscape.

There is pleasant walking beside the Mersey estuary, with surprisingly rural views.

There are attractive wooded stretches and, towards the end, a fine view across Budworth Pool of Little Budworth Church.

The views extend over the Cheshire plain and across to the hills of North Wales on this undulating walk to the south and east of Malpas.

From the heights of Mow Cop, you descend to the Macclesfield Canal and on across fields to Little Moreton Hall. Shorter version of walk 5½ miles (8.8km).

The first part of the walk is mainly through a secluded valley; much of the return leg is beside a canal.

A mixture of woodland and open moorland, with outstanding views, are the main ingredients of this superb Peak District walk that takes you to the distinctive summit of Shutlingsloe.

This route in the Peak District encompasses both the conifers of Macclesfield Forest and some rough moorland walking. The views are superb. Shorter version of walk 7½ miles (12km).

After walking across fields and beside a canal, the climb to the summit of The Cloud is a relatively easy one and the views are superb. Two shorter options available (see page 64).

A country park, picturesque village, canal and unique – and recently restored – boat lift create a walk of great interest and variety.

Easy walking along a disused railway track is followed by an invigorating stretch beside the Dee estuary. There are fine views looking across to North Wales.

On the final stretch, there are particularly memorable views looking across Big Mere to Marbury Church.

This lengthy but undemanding walk explores the pleasant and gently undulating countryside around the hilltop village of Wybunbury.

Introduction to Cheshire

The conventional image of the typical Cheshire landscape is of rich parklands, lazily meandering rivers, tree-fringed meres, attractive black-and-white villages with sandstone churches, and flat, lush pastures occupied by contented-looking cattle. And indeed this is a largely accurate picture of much of the county. This is the landscape that has made Cheshire a major dairy farming area, noted especially for its mild, crumbly cheese. But there are other sides to Cheshire and the county is far more varied than many people realise – it is undulating rather than flat, and there are hills, even rugged ones at that. Cheshire is a frontier county, not only in the obvious sense of being on the Welsh border but also as a frontier between south and north. Its rich pasturelands are similar to those of its neighbours to the south – Shropshire and Staffordshire – but its gritstone moors and northern industrial and commuter belt are more reminiscent of the textile country of Lancashire and Yorkshire.

Hill country

Outside the area it is perhaps not widely known that a slice of eastern Cheshire lies within the Peak District National Park. Here is a landscape of deep valleys, gritstone moors, isolated farms and stone hamlets that could not be farther removed from the typical picture of the county just described. This is Pennine Cheshire, virtually identical in appearance and spirit to the moorlands farther north in Yorkshire and Lancashire. Macclesfield is the chief centre of this part of the county and could hardly be more of a Pennine town with its skyline of silk mills and terrace houses.

Farther west – and visible from the gritstone moors of the Peak District – is another range of hills; the sandstone ridge which runs north to south across the central part of the county. These are lower and less rugged than the gritstone moors of the Peak District and largely covered with woodland but the ridge provides some surprisingly steep slopes and a number of fine viewpoints. In the south, this sandstone ridge drops gently to the Shropshire border but where it ends in the north, at the cliffs above Helsby and Frodsham, it falls away abruptly to the flat and heavily-industrialised country of the Mersey estuary.

Commuter country

Another side to Cheshire is the commuter-belt area, 'stockbroker country', in the north, serving Manchester, Liverpool and the adjacent towns. To the south of Stockport and Manchester are a collection of towns and villages that are among the most affluent in the country outside the Home Counties, but still with much attractive countryside between them. Farther west, between the Dee and the Mersey, is the Wirral peninsula, just across the river from Liverpool. Despite suburban expansion and industrialisaton on its eastern - Mersey-

From the summit of Nab Head

side, the Wirral still retains a sense of remoteness and isolation in places and has some good walking country. Particularly impressive are the views from its western side, looking across the marshlands of the Dee to the hills of North Wales.

County boundaries

The River Mersey was always the traditional and clearly-defined border between Cheshire and Lancashire but this changed in the local government reorganisation of 1974. Cheshire both gained and lost. It gained land around Warrington and Widnes, to the north of the Mersey, but lost lands in the Wirral and to the south of Manchester to the new metropolitan counties of Merseyside and Greater Manchester respectively.

For the purposes of this walking guide, Cheshire has been interpreted in the widest possible sense. Walks have been included in the former Cheshire areas of Merseyside and Greater Manchester, plus one to the north of the Mersey that was never in the traditional county.

Castles, forests and country houses

Cheshire is part of the Welsh border country and in the Middle Ages the earls of Chester were given almost royal powers in exchange for protecting this vulnerable area from Welsh raids. Castles such as Beeston, Chester and the vanished one at Malpas are reminders that for many centuries this was a warlike and unsettled area.

During the Middle Ages, a substantial part of northern Cheshire was covered by the great royal forests of Mara and Mondrum and largely given over to hunting. Subsequent fellings in the 17th and 18th centuries destroyed much of these forests but a fragment survives at Delamere – excellent walking country – and there are good wooded stretches in other parts of the county.

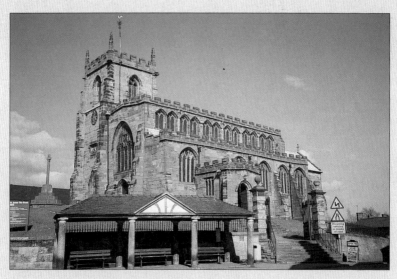

Audlem

The ending of the wars with the Welsh brought more peaceful and settled conditions and the subsequent agricultural prosperity was largely responsible for the handsome old towns, attractive villages and country houses for which the county is renowned. Of the latter, Little Moreton Hall is the most famous. Almost everyone has seen pictures of it on calendars and birthday cards as its picturesque appearance has made it one of the most photographed buildings in the country. It typifies Cheshire and has virtually become a symbol of the county. Other black-and-white houses are at Gawsworth and Bramhall and thousands of visitors flock to the great houses and parklands of Lyme, Adlington, Tatton and Dunham Massey, many now in the ownership of the National Trust.

Chester

The principal tourist attraction in Cheshire is the county town, the great historic city of Chester, one of England's oldest, most attractive and most distinctive cities. Originally the Roman fort of Deva, it has been a major port, fortress, base for English incursions into Wales, administrative centre and cathedral city. Its circuit of walls is virtually intact – and make a superb urban walk – and within them are the city's main historic and architectural attractions. Unique to Chester are the Rows, two-storeyed covered walkways, with shops at both street and upper level. Why these are found nowhere else has never been satisfactorily explained but it is known that they correspond with the limits of the Roman fort.

Canals and railway tracks

Although primarily an agricultural county, the Industrial Revolution did not entirely pass Cheshire by. Proximity to Manchester ensured that north-east Cheshire became part of the textile belt and the county shared with Lancashire the later chemical industries of Merseyside. Birkenhead, chief town of the Wirral, rivalled its near neighbour, Liverpool, as a port and important centre for shipbuilding. A legacy of this which is particularly relevant to walkers is the extensive canal network. There are four main canals - Macclesfield, Trent and Mersey, Bridgewater and Shropshire Union - and they were constructed both to serve Cheshire's own industries and agriculture and to provide a link between the industries and agriculture and to provide a link between the industrial Midlands and the Mersey. Their towpaths now make excellent walking routes, tranquil and scenic.

Another legacy of the Industrial Revolution is a number of disused railway tracks and some of these are featured in the selection of walks. The long-distance Wirral Way is based entirely around a railway line which ran along the western side of the Wirral.

Walking in the area

Cheshire has a large number of clearly-waymarked long distance routes. The principal ones are the Wirral Way and the Sandstone and Gritstone Trails. The latter two run, for the most part, in a roughly north-south direction along the ridges of the sandstone hills of central Cheshire and the gritstone hills and moors of the Peak District respectively. Stretches of the South Cheshire Way, Bollin Valley Way, Marches Way, Dane Valley Way and Delamere Way are also featured in the following routes.

So if walkers come to Cheshire expecting a wholly flat county, they are in for something of a surprise. There are plenty of easy, gently undulating and undemanding walks that take you across a typical Cheshire landscape and these are most enjoyable, invariably passing through some of the attractive villages and by some of the county's outstanding churches or country houses. But you can also experience rough and challenging moorland hikes on the edge of the Peak District, plenty of attractive woodland walks along the sandstone

Shropshire Union Canal near Beeston Castle

ridge, or across parklands, or through the remnants of the medieval forests, a superb choice of peaceful canal walks and, on the Wirral, even coastal – or at least estuary – walking.

Little Budworth Country Park

Start	Little Budworth Country Park car park, about ½ mile (800m) to the west of Little Budworth
Distance	4 miles (6.4km)
Approximate time	2 hours
Parking	Little Budworth Country Park
Refreshments	Pubs at Little Budworth
Ordnance Survey maps	Explorer 267 (Northwich & Delamere Forest), Landranger 117 (Chester & Wrexham)

The first half of this easy walk is through the attractive woodlands of Little Budworth Country Park, a fragment of the great medieval forests of Mara and Mondrum. Later comes more open country and, towards the end, there is a memorable view of the tower of Little Budworth Church, rising above Budworth Pool. This could be a noisy walk on days when there is racing at nearby Oulton Park.

Turn left out of the car park – either along the road or cross over and take the parallel path through the trees – to a T-junction and turn right. Immediately bear left through the trees to pick up a path which keeps by the perimeter of Oulton Park racing circuit on the left. Cross a drive by the entrance to Oulton Park, keep ahead and the path emerges onto the road **A**.

Cross over and walk along a track which keeps along the left edge of woodland. Across the fields to the left are views towards the slopes of Delamere Forest. At a crossways, turn right **B** along an enclosed track which continues through woodland to a road. Cross over, take the lane opposite, passing another country park car park, and at a public footpath sign to Whitehall Lane and Coach Road, turn right along a track by the left edge of woodland **C**.

After passing to the right of a house, head down to climb a stile, keep to the left of a pool and the path continues through trees to a fork. Take the left-hand path and just beyond a purple arrow waymark, turn left onto a path which keeps parallel to the left edge of the wood. On emerging onto a track, continue along it, downhill, curving left in front of a house and passing to the right of a pond to reach a crossways. Keep ahead, curving right and heading gently uphill, and just before the track becomes tarmac, turn right along an enclosed tarmac track **D**.

Where this track bends right, bear left along a hedge-lined track to a T-junction and turn right along another enclosed track to a road. Turn right, almost immediately turn left **E** onto a broad track and later the way continues along a narrower enclosed path. Look

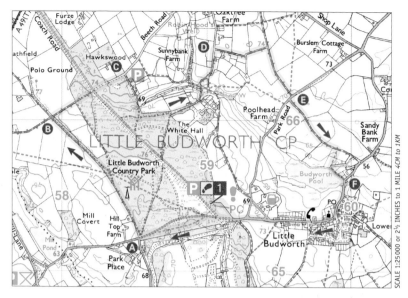

| 0 | 200 | 400 | 600 | 800 METRES | 1 |
| 0 | 200 | 400 | 600 YARDS | ½ | |

KILOMETRES
MILES

out for a public footpath sign where you turn right over a stile and walk across two fields, climbing a stile, towards Budworth Pool. After climbing a stile on the far side of the second field, turn left along a path beside the pool. From here there is a particularly attractive view of Little Budworth Church on the other side of the water.

Climb a stile onto a road, turn right **F** and follow the road as it bends right through the village, passing to the left of the church. This mostly dates from the late 18th century, apart from the 16th-century tower. Keep ahead and about 100 yds (91m) beyond the second road on the right, bear right onto a path which leads through trees back to the car park and then the starting point of the walk.

Pool and church at Little Budworth

Wirswall Hill and Big Mere

Start	Marbury
Distance	3½ miles (5.6km)
Approximate time	2 hours
Parking	Roadside parking at Marbury
Refreshments	Pub at Marbury
Ordnance Survey maps	Explorer 257 (Crewe & Nantwich), Landranger 117 (Chester & Wrexham)

A pleasant stroll across fields and along a lane is followed by a short and easy climb up the slopes of Wirswall Hill, 512 ft (156m) high. The return leg is along the well-waymarked South Cheshire Way and, on the descent into Marbury, both the extensive vistas over the Cheshire plain and the nearer views looking across Big Mere to Marbury Church are outstanding.

Marbury's 15th-century sandstone church occupies a superb site above Big Mere, the larger of the two meres around this peaceful and remote village. The walk begins in the village centre by the green and Swan Inn. Turn along Wirswall Road and at a public footpath sign, turn left over a stile and walk across a field to another stile.

Big Mere and Marbury

Climb it and continue in the same direction across the next field, veering slightly right after passing a redundant stile to cross a footbridge on the far side. Bear left to climb a stile, bear right to follow a path across a field and, after crossing a plank footbridge, the path bends right. Look out for where you turn left over a stile, head gently uphill across a field and climb a stile onto a lane Ⓐ. Turn left along this narrow

winding lane for $\frac{1}{2}$ mile (800m) and by the Wirswall sign, turn left along a track to a public footpath sign and turn right over a stile **B**.

Keep ahead to climb the slopes of Wirswall Hill, passing between two sets of redundant gateposts, and at the top, climb a stile onto the lane again. Turn left, follow the lane around a right bend and at a public footpath sign, turn left along a fence-lined track **C** to join the South Cheshire Way. You keep along it for the remainder of the walk. Follow the track around a left bend, pass between farm buildings and, at a fork, take the right hand track. Go through a gate, where the track curves left keep ahead to climb a stile and continue along the right edge of a field.

At a fingerpost by a stile on the right, turn left **D** – in the Marbury direction – and head gently uphill across a field to a stile. Climb the stile, keep ahead to go through a gate, head diagonally across

the next field and at the bottom end, climb two stiles in quick succession. Walk along the right edge of a field, climb a stile, veer slightly left through a shallow valley, passing an isolated waymarked tree, and continue across the uneven field, heading down to the left corner of woodland to reach a stile. Climb it and as you walk along the right edge of a field by woodland on the right, the views ahead of Big Mere and Marbury Church are particularly memorable.

Climb a stile in the field corner, keep ahead along a tree-lined path beside the mere, climb another stile and continue beside the mere. After climbing the next stile, turn right away from the water, head across the field to go through a gate onto a lane and turn left to the starting point of the walk. ●

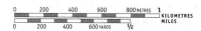

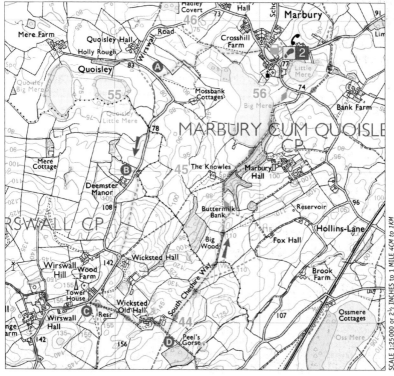

Hale and the Mersey estuary

Start	Hale
Distance	5 miles (8km)
Approximate time	2½ hours
Parking	Roadside parking in centre of Hale
Refreshments	Pubs at Hale
Ordnance Survey maps	Explorer 275 (Liverpool), Landranger 108 (Liverpool)

Industry is not far way – visible both up and down the river and on the opposite side – but this is an unexpectedly pleasant, green and peaceful walk. The opening stretch is across fields, the last part is along lanes and roads but most of the route is beside the Mersey estuary. There are fine views across the river to the sandstone ridge above Helsby and Frodsham and the Clwydian hills of North Wales are visible on the horizon.

The church, spacious Victorian villas and attractive thatched cottages of Hale are set in a rural oasis near the north bank of the River Mersey, sandwiched between Widnes and Liverpool and close to Liverpool Airport. In the 19th century, the village became a popular residence for wealthy Liverpool

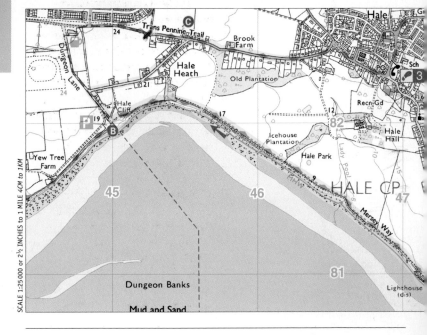

SCALE 1:25000 or 2½ INCHES to 1 MILE 4CM to 1KM

merchants, hence the grand houses. A famous earlier resident was John Middleton, known as the 'Childe of Hale', a nine-foot giant who lived from 1578 to 1623 and was a favourite at the court of James I. He is buried in the churchyard of the mainly 18th-century church.

📷 Start at the road junction by the war memorial in the village centre and walk along Church End, passing to the left of the Childe of Hale pub and the cottage in which John Middleton lived. Just before reaching the church, turn left along Within Way, follow the lane around right and left bends, and it later degenerates into a rough track. To the left, the bridge over the Mersey that links Widnes and Runcorn can be seen.

Hale Lighthouse

Where the track ends, go through a kissing-gate, at a public footpath sign to Hale Lighthouse, and keep ahead along a path towards the river. At a Mersey Way post, turn right through a kissing-gate **A** and continue along a path beside the estuary to the disused lighthouse at Hale Head where you go through another kissing-gate onto a track. Go through the kissing-gate opposite and continue beside the estuary along the top of low cliffs. Across the fields to the right, Hale church tower can be seen. The path goes through two more kissing-gates and at one point, turns left to cross a footbridge.

At Hale Cliff descend steps, continue through trees, cross a footbridge and ascend steps to regain the clifftop. Keep ahead and the path gently descends through woodland again to a T-junction **B**. Turn right, in the Speke direction, go through a kissing-gate and continue to a lane. Keep ahead – Liverpool Airport is to the left – take the first lane on the right and at a T-junction **C**, turn right into Hale. Follow the road around a right bend to return to the start. ●

Bollington and Nab Head

Start	Bollington, Middlewood Way car park
Distance	3½ miles (5.6km) Shorter version 2½ miles (4km)
Approximate time	2 hours (1½ hours for shorter walk)
Parking	Bollington
Refreshments	Pubs at Bollington, pub at Whiteley Green
Ordnance Survey maps	Explorer 268 (Wilmslow, Macclesfield & Congleton), Landranger 118 (Stoke-on-Trent & Macclesfield)

You begin by climbing steps onto a viaduct and the first part of the walk – just over ½ mile (800m) – is along a disused railway track. A combination of lanes, tracks and field paths leads to the base of Nab Head and this is followed by a short and relatively undemanding climb to the summit, 935 ft (285m) high and a magnificent viewpoint over the Cheshire plain. The shorter walk omits Nab Head and returns directly to Bollington.

With its stone houses, Victorian churches and chapels, mill buildings, aqueduct and railway viaduct, there is a real Pennine feel about Bollington.

Begin by turning right onto a path which passes under the viaduct and bends right to a gate. Go through, climb the steps beside the viaduct and at the top, bear left along a track. This was the former track of the Macclesfield to Marple railway, now converted into the

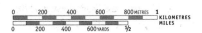

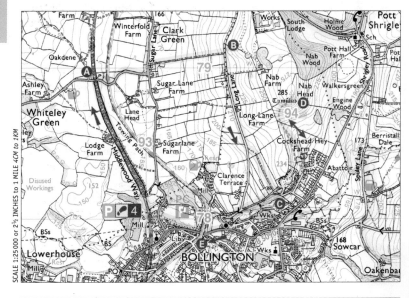

Middlewood Way, a footpath and cycle way. Walk through a tree-lined cutting, pass under one bridge and in front of the second one, turn left up steps to a lane **Ⓐ**. The pub at Whiteley Green is to the left but the route continues to the right over the bridge. Keep ahead to cross a bridge over the Macclesfield Canal and follow the lane to a T-junction. Turn left and at a public footpath sign, turn right over a stile, beside a Methodist church, and walk along an enclosed track to another

Moorland near Bollington

stile. After climbing it, head uphill along the right edge of two fields, passing through a hedge gap, and climb a stile onto a lane **Ⓑ**.

Turn right along this narrow lane and after almost ½ mile (800m), turn left over a stone stile, at a public footpath sign, and walk across a field to climb another stone stile. Continue along the right edge of the next field, go through a gate in the corner, descend steps to a track and turn right to a public footpath sign **Ⓒ**.

Keep ahead for the short walk, following route directions after the next time point **Ⓒ** *appears in the text.*

For the full walk, turn sharp left along a walled track, descending steps, and continue in front of cottages down to a road. Turn left along Cocksheadhey Road – it later becomes a rough track – at a public footpath sign, keep ahead through a gate, walk along a paved track and in front of a gate, turn right over a stone stile. Keep ahead to climb another stile, cross a track and follow a well-worn and well-waymarked path uphill across grass to a ladder stile in the top left-hand corner of a field.

Climb it, continue uphill along the left edge of the next field and after passing redundant gateposts, bear right away from the field edge and head steeply uphill to the triangulation pillar on the summit of Nab Head **Ⓓ**. In clear conditions, the views from here are spectacular and extensive, stretching across Macclesfield, Bollington and the Cheshire plain to Alderley Edge and the distant outline of Helsby Hill. The line of the Pennines and the hills of the Peak District can also be seen.

Retrace your steps to point **Ⓒ** to rejoin the shorter walk and turn left downhill along a walled tarmac track. On joining a lane, keep ahead steeply downhill, bending sharply to the left and continuing down to a road in Bollington. Turn right and, after going under the canal aqueduct, turn right into a park **Ⓔ**. Turn left down steps, cross a footbridge over a stream and keep ahead beside it to join a tarmac path. Bear right, descend steps to recross the stream and the path bends left to continue through the park to a road opposite the car park. ●

Dane Valley

Start	Brereton Heath Country Park
Distance	5 miles (8km)
Approximate time	2½ hours
Parking	Brereton Heath Country Park
Refreshments	Pub at Swettenham
Ordnance Survey maps	Explorer 268 (Wilmslow, Macclesfield & Congleton), Landranger 118 (Stoke-on-Trent & Macclesfield)

The route descends into the attractive valley of the meandering River Dane and continues on to the small and secluded village of Swettenham. After a circuit around the village, you retrace your steps to the start. In spring, it is worthwhile making a short detour through Daffodil Dell, the steep-sided wooded valley of Swettenham Brook just to the east of the village, where the thousands of daffodils make a glorious sight.

Brereton Heath Country Park, an attractive area of grassland, woodland and lake, was created from a former sand quarry. 🔦 Facing the lake, turn left along a path which passes to the left of the information centre and just before the path bends right – at a notice 'No Horses or Motor Cycles' – bear left across grass. Turn left in front of a fence and climb a stile onto a lane.

Turn right and at a T-junction, **Ⓐ**

Daffodil Dell near Swettenham

keep ahead along a tarmac track – there are public bridleway and Dane Valley Way signs here – to a gate. Go through, continue along the drive to Davenport Hall and at a fork, take the right hand drive which winds gently downhill into the lovely Dane valley. Go through a gate, cross a bridge over the River Dane and keep ahead along the track. After going through a gate, continue along a narrow lane which winds gently uphill into Swettenham. The church, a curious but harmonious mixture of styles, dates from the Middle Ages but was mainly rebuilt in brick in the early 18th century.

At a public footpath sign opposite the church, turn right **Ⓑ** over a stile and walk along an enclosed path to another stile. Climb it, continue along the right edge of a field and at a fence corner, keep straight ahead, making for another fence corner, and then continue along the left field edge to a stile. Climb it, keep along the left edge of the next two

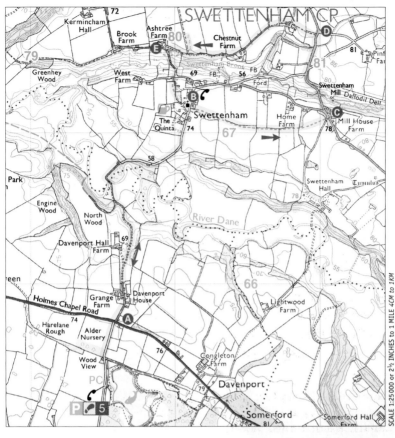

SCALE 1:25 000 or 2½ INCHES to 1 MILE 4CM to 1KM

0	200	400	600	800 METRES
0	200	400	600 YARDS	½

1 KILOMETRES MILES

fields, climbing more stiles, and where the fence and track bend left in the third field, keep straight ahead and climb a stile on the far side onto a tarmac drive.

Bear left to a road **C**, turn left and at a fork immediately ahead, take the right hand road (Congleton Road). *At this point, a detour to the right through a nursery – there is a modest fee – enables you to visit the wooded Daffodil Dell. This is definitely to be recommended in springtime as the display of daffodils is magnificent.*

The route continues along Congleton Road, crossing Swettenham Brook, and just before the road curves left, turn left over a stile **D**, at a public footpath sign, and walk along the right edge of a field. Look out for where you turn right over

a stile, turn left and follow a fence on the left to another stile. After climbing that one, keep ahead along a tarmac drive, climb a stile, continue along the left edge of a field and climb a stile in the corner. Bear left along an attractive, tree-lined enclosed track and opposite Ashtree Farm, turn sharp left beside a gate **E** onto an enclosed, sunken wooded path which descends to cross a bridge over Swettenham Brook.

Head steeply uphill to a track, turn right and almost immediately turn left over a stile, at a public footpath sign, and walk along the left edge of a field. In the corner turn left over a stile and walk along an enclosed track to emerge onto a tarmac track in front of Swettenham Church. Bear right to a lane, **B** turn right, here picking up the outward route, and retrace your steps to the start.

DANE VALLEY ● 21

Around Kelsall

Start	Gresty's Waste car park, off A54
Distance	5 miles (8km)
Approximate time	2½ hours
Parking	Gresty's Waste
Refreshments	Pub at Kelsall, café at point **F**
Ordnance Survey maps	Explorer 267 (Northwich & Delamere Forest), Landranger 117 (Chester & Wrexham)

This attractive walk is on the southern fringes of Delamere Forest and the first and last parts are through woodland. Most of the route is across open country and, from the higher points, there are fine and extensive views, especially looking towards the hills of North Wales on the horizon.

Start by taking the path through the trees, at a Sandstone Trail sign, that leads off from the car park and runs parallel to the A54. At a fingerpost, turn right to cross the road and continue along a track through Nettleford Wood, part of Delamere Forest. Head gently uphill through the trees to another fingerpost and turn left, **A** in the Yeld Lane direction.

After passing beside a barrier, keep ahead along a lane (Forest Gate Lane) to a T-junction and turn left along Yeld Lane. Head downhill, crossing a bridge over the A54, and at a crossroads turn right **B** along a road through Kelsall. After about ½ mile (800m) – opposite a church on the right – turn left, **C** at a public footpath sign, along an enclosed path. Follow the path around right and left bends to a road, turn left and take the first road on the right (Kingswood Walk).

Where the road ends, go up steps and keep ahead along an enclosed track to a road. Cross over, continue along Elizabeth Close and where the road bends right, keep ahead, at a public footpath sign, along an uphill, enclosed tarmac path. Continue up a flight of steps, go through a kissing-gate at the top, walk along the left edge of a field and go through another kissing-gate onto a lane **D**.

Immediately turn right along a tarmac track, soon bearing right off it across grass to a public footpath sign to Willinghton, and

Above Kelsall

continue through trees to a kissing-gate. Go through, keep along the left edge of the next three fields, climbing two stiles, and in the corner of the last field, turn left over a stile and descend steps. Now comes a most attractive part of the walk as you continue downhill along the left side of a valley below steeply sloping woodland. At the bottom, keep ahead along a track which eventually emerges onto a lane **E**. Turn left uphill along this winding lane, take the first lane on the right (Tirley Lane) and where it bends right, turn left, **F** at a public footpath sign, along an enclosed track beside Summertree Tea Room. The rest of the walk is on the well-waymarked Sandstone Trail.

Go through a kissing-gate, keep along the right edge of the next two fields, climbing a stile, but before reaching the corner of the second field, turn right

through a kissing-gate. Turn left to continue downhill along the left edge of the next field, climb a stile in the bottom corner, descend steps and turn left along a path. At a Sandstone Trail post, turn right and at a T-junction, turn left along a well-surfaced woodland track. Where the track bends left, keep ahead along an uphill sandy path to a T-junction and turn right **G**. Following the regular waymarks, walk along a path which heads downhill and continues to a stile. Climb it, and another one immediately in front, and continue along a winding path which heads downhill again to cross a footbridge over a brook. Ascend steps and at the top, turn right to return to the car park. ●

SCALE 1:25 000 or 2½ INCHES to 1 MILE 4CM to 1KM

Astbury Mere and village

Start	Astbury Mere Country Park, on southern edge of Congleton and signposted from the A34
Distance	5½ miles (8.8km)
Approximate time	2½ hours
Parking	Astbury Mere Country Park
Refreshments	Pub at Astbury
Ordnance Survey maps	Explorer 268 (Wilmslow, Macclesfield & Congleton), Landranger 118 (Stoke-on-Trent & Macclesfield)

From the shores of Astbury Mere on the southern outskirts of Congleton, the route proceeds mainly via enclosed tracks and paths to the Macclesfield Canal. After a pleasant walk beside the canal, field paths bring you into the attractive village of Astbury and, for much of the route, the tower and spire of its imposing church are in sight.

Begin by taking the well-surfaced path which leads from the front of the visitor centre down to the lake and then bends left to continue beside it. At a fork by the corner of the lake, take the left hand uphill path, climb steps, keep ahead and turn right to climb more steps to a T-junction.

Turn right and the path bends left, becomes enclosed and continues above the mere before descending to a lane. Turn left **A** and, at a public footpath sign, turn right along an enclosed path. *If this path is muddy and overgrown, walkers might prefer to use the parallel track.* The path emerges onto this track and you continue along it, curving right. In front of a farm, turn sharp left **B** through a gate and walk along an attractive, tree-lined path, crossing a footbridge over a brook, to reach a gate.

Go through, keep ahead along a well-surfaced, tree-lined track and just after going through another gate, turn right and descend steps to the towpath of the Macclesfield Canal **C**. Turn right, keep

beside the canal for 1¼ miles (2km) and at Watery Lane Aqueduct, turn right over a stile **D**. This can be difficult to spot but it is about halfway between bridges 80 and 81. Head down to climb another stile and descend steps to a lane. Turn left and where the lane curves left, turn right over a stile, at a public footpath sign, and keep ahead to cross a plank footbridge over a brook.

Immediately bear left across a rather uneven field to a stile, climb it and walk along the right edge of the next field. Climb a stile, head across the field to climb a stile in the far right-hand corner and continue along the right edge of the next two fields. At a fence corner, turn right over a stile, bear right and head down across a field to climb another stile. Keep ahead across the next field – there are farm buildings to the left – and in the far left hand corner, climb a stile onto a road **E**. Turn left into Astbury.

With an imposing late medieval church and brick and half-timbered

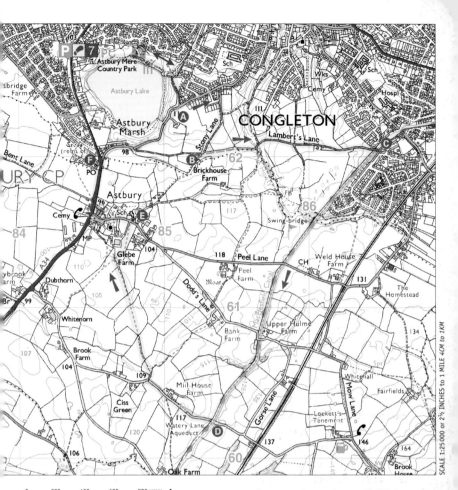

SCALE 1:25 000 or 2½ INCHES to 1 MILE 4CM to 1KM

0	200	400	600	800 METRES	1

KILOMETRES
MILES

0	200	400	600 YARDS	½

cottages grouped around a green, Astbury is a particularly attractive village. The sandstone church is one of the finest in Cheshire and has a curious design; the tower and spire stand at the north-west corner of the church and are almost detached from it. The interior is spacious and impressive, with a wide nave and some fine wood carving.

At a fork by the church, take the right-hand road alongside the village green to the A34 and turn right.

Turn right again along a lane called Fol Hollow **F** and just before the first of the houses, turn left, at a public footpath sign, **A** along an enclosed path. Here you pick up the outward route and retrace your steps to the start.

Astbury

Chester and the River Dee

Start	Chester, The Cross
Distance	5 miles (8km)
Approximate time	2½ hours
Parking	Chester
Refreshments	Pubs and cafés at Chester
Ordnance Survey maps	Explorer 266 (Wirral & Chester), Landranger 117 (Chester & Wrexham)

This flat and easy walk to the south of Chester falls into two distinct halves. Much of the first half is through attractive woodland and the return leg is across meadows bordering the River Dee. The route uses short stretches of Chester's medieval walls and passes some of the city's historic sites but allow plenty of time for a thorough exploration of one of England's most attractive, historic and fascinating cities.

Throughout its long history Chester has played many roles. Originally the Roman fort of Deva, it has been a major port (until the Dee silted up), both a defensive fortress against the Welsh and a springboard for English invasions of Wales, administrative centre and cathedral city.

Although none of the original gateways survive, Chester retains its circuit of medieval walls and most of its historic and architectural attractions lie within the walls. Foremost among these are the castle and cathedral. Of Chester's medieval castle, one of the principal fortresses along the Welsh border, only the 13th-century Agricola Tower remains. Most of it was pulled down in the late 18th and early 19th centuries and replaced by imposing classical buildings to serve as barracks and law court. Chester Cathedral was originally a Benedictine abbey, raised to cathedral status by Henry VIII in 1541 after the dissolution of the monasteries.

The cloisters and other monastic buildings on the north side of the church are among its principal assets. Also worth seeing are the superb and intricately-carved 14th-century choir stalls, among the finest in the country. Most of the cathedral dates from the 14th and 15th centuries and it was heavily restored in the Victorian era.

Unique to Chester are the Rows, a series of covered walkways. These are medieval in origin, are found in the four main streets which radiate from The Cross and roughly correspond to the area originally enclosed by the Roman walls. Although their picturesque black-and-white appearance is more Victorian than Tudor, this in no way detracts from their appeal and attractiveness.

From The Cross, walk down Bridge Street and on down Lower Bridge Street, passing under Bridgegate to reach the Old Dee Bridge. Immediately turn right along Castle Drive and after passing County Hall, you can either continue along the road or take to the medieval walls, passing below the buildings of Chester Castle, to a main road. Cross over, turn left to cross Grosvenor Bridge and then bear right **A** through a gap in the railings onto a path which descends through woodland, bending right to meet another path.

Turn left to continue through the trees and the path rises to emerge onto a road at a busy junction. Cross four roads in quick succession, curving left all the time, to reach Wrexham Road. Turn right and then immediately turn left along a tarmac path to a T-junction to the right of ornamental gates and in front of a lodge **B**. Turn right onto an attractive tarmac track which continues

through woodland. This is the Chester Approach, a driveway constructed to link the Duke of Westminster's residence of Eaton Hall with Chester. After ¾ mile (1.2km), look out for a ladder stile on the left at the corner of a wood. Do not climb it but a few yards farther on, turn left **C** along a path which keeps by the left inside edge of the wood. At a fork, take the right-hand path which continues through the trees and pass beside a fence onto a road.

Turn sharp right and at a public footpath sign, turn left **D** over a stile and walk along the left edge of a field, descending an embankment to reach

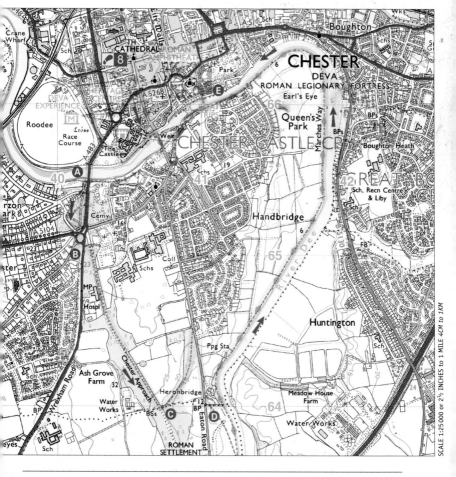

SCALE 1:25 000 or 2½ INCHES to 1 MILE 4CM to 1KM

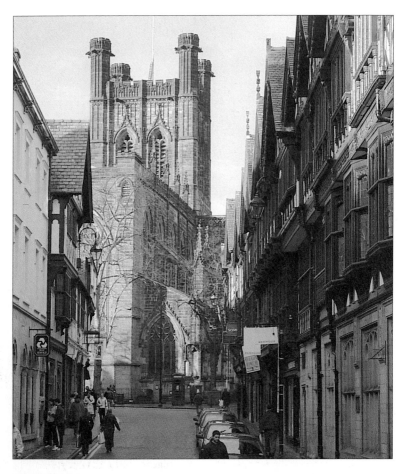

Chester Cathedral

the River Dee. Turn left over a stile and follow an attractive riverside path back to Chester, a distance of about 2$\frac{1}{4}$ miles (3.6km). The path keeps along the edge of meadows, via a series of stiles, and follows the river around a left bend. In the corner of the final meadow, go through a kissing-gate and keep ahead along a paved path to a suspension footbridge **E**.

Immediately after going under the bridge, turn left up a flight of steps and turn left at the top to cross the bridge. There are fine views both up and down the river. On the other side, keep ahead up more steps and walk along a paved path which curves left by the wall of

St John's Church on the left. This majestic and partly ruined Norman church briefly served as the cathedral of the Mercian diocese in the late 11th century. Keep ahead along Little St John Street, passing to the right of the Roman amphitheatre, built towards the end of the 1st century AD, and on reaching Newgate climb steps onto the walls.

Cross Newgate and keep along the walls as far as Eastgate, which is surmounted by a distinctive clock tower, erected in 1897 to commemorate Queen Victoria's Diamond Jubilee. Here you descend from the walls, turn right to pass under the gate and walk along Eastgate Street back to the start. ●

Sandbach

Start	Sandbach
Distance	6 miles (9.6km)
Approximate time	3 hours
Parking	Sandbach
Refreshments	Pubs and cafés at Sandbach, pub and café at Hassall Green, pubs at Wheelock
Ordnance Survey maps	Explorer 268 (Wilmslow, Macclesfield & Congleton), Landranger 118 (Stoke-on-Trent & Macclesfield)

You escape surprisingly quickly from the bustle of Sandbach town centre and busy main roads into a tranquil, wooded and secluded valley. After an inevitably noisier stretch close to the M6, most of the return leg is equally peaceful, first beside the Trent and Mersey Canal between Hassall Green and Wheelock, and finally through another secluded valley on the edge of the town.

The walk starts in the town centre by the Sandbach Crosses, a pair of carved 9th-century Anglo-Saxon crosses. Walk towards the war memorial and turn left down High Street, passing to the right of the large and handsome church, built mainly in 1633 and restored in the Victorian era.

At a crossroads cross the busy A534, turn right Ⓐ along it and just after crossing a side road, bear left across grass to pick up a path and follow it to a T-junction in front of a brook. Turn left and just before the path rises towards houses, turn right to climb a stile, bear left and head uphill along the left edge of a field. Climb a stile, keep ahead to climb another one and continue along an enclosed track to a lane Ⓑ.

Turn left, turn right at a T-junction and at a public footpath sign, turn left along an enclosed track Ⓒ. Where the track curves right at a waymarked post, bear left onto a path by the left edge of

a field and at a hedge corner, the path veers slightly right, continues downhill and descends steps to cross a footbridge over a brook. Continue uphill along the right edge of a field, go through a kissing-gate, keep ahead to go through another, cross a track and go through another kissing-gate. Turn right along a path, go through yet another kissing-gate, keep ahead by a fence on the right, climb a stile and pass to the left of a house. The path descends into a beautiful wooded dell to a stile to the left of a bridge.

Cross a track, go through the kissing-gate opposite and keep ahead beside a brook, climbing another stile. Look out for where you turn right to cross a footbridge over the brook, head uphill and continue across a field – there is a worn path – to a stile. After climbing it, veer slightly right across the next field, climb a stile on the far side, keep ahead to climb another and turn left **D** along a lane to cross a bridge over the M6.

At a public footpath sign, turn sharp right over a stile – doubling back along a path – turn left over another stile and walk along the right edge of a field parallel to the motorway. Climb a stile, keep ahead and the field edge bears left away from the M6. In the corner turn left to continue along the right edge and look out for where you turn right over a stile. Walk along an enclosed path which emerges onto a road in Hassall Green, keep ahead and at a fork, take the left hand road along the side of a square. Follow the road to the right, keep ahead to a T-junction, **E** turn right and after crossing a canal bridge, turn right onto the towpath of the Trent and Mersey Canal **F**.

Keep beside the canal, passing under the motorway, for about $1\frac{3}{4}$ miles (2.8km) to Wheelock. Just before reaching bridge 154, bear left up to a road **G**. Turn right to cross the bridge, immediately turn right down steps, at a

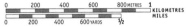

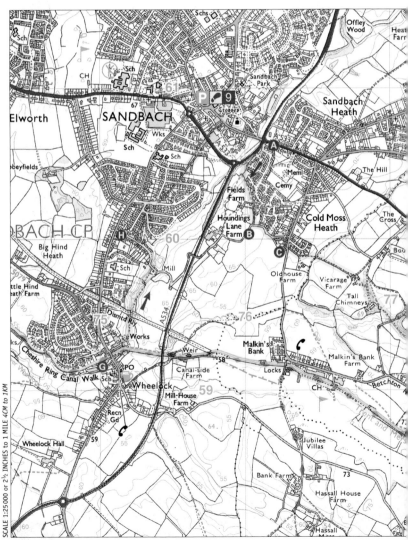

public footpath sign to Mill Hill Lane, and walk back along the other side of the canal as far as a waymarked post. Turn left here onto a path through woodland, turn right to cross a footbridge over a brook and turn left

Near Sandbach

alongside it, passing under a former railway bridge.

Climb a stile, keep ahead to climb another one and bear slightly left to continue along the bottom edge of a slopng field. Turn left to cross a brook and the path bears right and winds through trees to a narrow lane. Turn left uphill and shortly after passing Mill Hill Drive on the right, turn right, **H** at a public footpath sign, and walk along an enclosed path which bends right to emerge onto a road. Turn left, turn left again at a T-junction, turn right at the next T-junction and turn right again at another T-junction.

Take the first road on the left (Price Avenue) and almost immediately bear right along an enclosed track (Price Drive). Keep ahead in a straight line along a series of tracks and paths –crossing several roads (including a main road near Safeways) – to return directly to the start. ●

Delamere Forest

Start	Linmere, Forestry Commission car park
Distance	6 miles (9.6km)
Approximate time	3 hours
Parking	Linmere
Refreshments	Café at Delamere Forest Visitor Centre
Ordnance Survey maps	Explorer 267 (Northwich & Delamere Forest), Landranger 117 (Chester & Wrexham)

Apart from a middle stretch across open country, much of the walk is along clear, well-surfaced paths and tracks through the attractive woodlands of Delamere Forest, the 'Forest of the Meres'. Nowadays the forest is mainly coniferous and is a fragment of the great forests of Mara and Mondrum that covered much of Cheshire during the Middle Ages, but it still retains some impressive broadleaved trees and is popular walking country.

Originally the hunting ground of the powerful earls of Chester, the adjacent forests of Mara and Mondrum became a royal possession in the 14th century when Edward III took over the earldom.

Delamere Forest

They occupied most of the area between Nantwich and the River Mersey but extensive felling in the 17th and 18th centuries considerably reduced the area of woodland, and the present Delamere Forest comprises about 2400 acres (970ha).

With your back to the visitor centre, turn right along a track which keeps mainly along the left edge of woodland. After passing beside a barrier, keep ahead along an enclosed track and continue along a lane to a T-junction **A**. Turn right, follow the lane around a left bend and at a fork, take the right hand lane, which is signposted to Mouldsworth and Ashton. Keep ahead at a cross-roads and just before

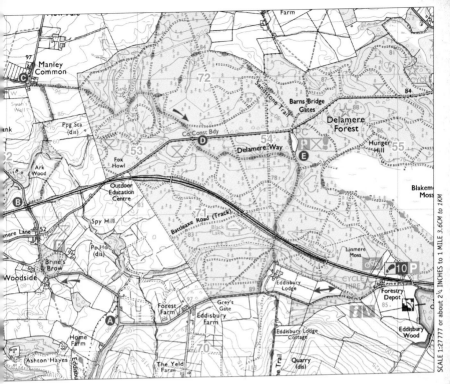

SCALE 1:27 777 or about 2½ INCHES to 1 MILE 3.6CM to 1KM

```
0     200    400    600   800 METRES  1
                                      KILOMETRES
                                      MILES
0     200    400    600 YARDS  ½
```

reaching a railway bridge, bear right along a track – there is an Eddisbury Way sign – climb a stile and pass under the bridge to another stile **B**.

After climbing it, turn right along the right edge of a field below the railway embankment and after about 100 yds (91m), bear left and head diagonally across the field to a stile. Climb it and head downhill across the next field, making for the left hand bottom corner where you climb a stile and cross a footbridge over a brook. Head uphill, keep along the left edge of a field and follow the edge as it curves right to a stile. Climb it, walk along the right edge of steeply sloping woodland to climb another stile and continue along the left edge of a field.

At an Eddisbury Way sign, turn left through a hedge gap, walk along the right edge of a field, turn left in the corner to continue along the right edge and climb a stile onto a lane **C**. Turn sharp right to double back along a parallel enclosed path – now on the Sandstone Trail – pass beside a barrier and continue along the track into the forest. The remainder of the walk is through woodland. Turn left at a T-junction, at the next T-junction turn left again and at a junction of tracks, turn right, here temporarily leaving the Sandstone Trail to join the Delamere Way.

Walk along a well-waymarked and well-surfaced track to a road **D**, cross over and continue along the broad track opposite. Keep along the main forest track to a crossways and turn right **E** to rejoin the Sandstone Trail. Follow the regular Sandstone Trail waymarks, crossing a railway bridge, and after going through a fence gap, the way continues along a path and through another fence gap onto a track. Turn left, here picking up the outward route, and retrace your steps to the start. ●

Audlem and the Shropshire Union Canal

Start	Audlem
Distance	6 miles (9.6km)
Approximate time	3 hours
Parking	Audlem
Refreshments	Pubs and café at Audlem
Ordnance Survey maps	Explorer 257 (Crewe & Nantwich), Landranger 118 (Stoke on-Trent & Macclesfield)

This route is in the attractive valley of the River Weaver in south Cheshire, not far from the Shropshire border. An opening stretch across fields is followed by a pleasant and peaceful 2-mile (3.2-km) walk along the towpath of the Shropshire Union Canal. There are fine and extensive views throughout.

The Square in the centre of the attractive and unassuming village of Audlem is dominated by the imposing, mainly 15th-century church. Below the church is the Shambles, a 17th-century market cross.

Start in The Square and walk along Stafford Street, passing to the right of the church. Opposite School Lane, turn left **A** along a lane and where it bends left, keep ahead along a track (Mill Lane). Continue along this enclosed track which eventually bends left to emerge onto a lane. Turn left and where the lane

River Weaver near Audlem

bends left, turn right, **B** at a public footpath sign, along the tarmac drive to The Parkes. Just before reaching gateposts, bear left to climb a stile, walk along the left edge of a field and go through a kissing-gate onto a road.

Turn left and almost immediately turn right up steps, climb a stile and keep along the right edge of a field. In the corner turn left, turn right over a stile into the next field, turn right again and turn left to continue along the right field edge. In the next corner turn left again, turn right through a gate, keep ahead to go through another gate and continue along a track, passing to the left of farm buildings. Keep ahead along a narrow lane and where the tarmac ends, turn left over a stile to join the South Cheshire Way **C**.

Walk along the left edge of a field, climb a stile, keep ahead along an enclosed path and after climbing the next stile, the route continues along the right edge of a field. Head gently

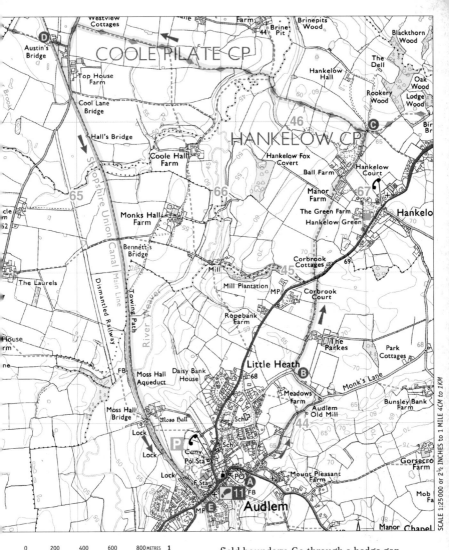

downhill along a track which curves right and immediately after crossing a bridge over the River Weaver, turn left alongside it to a stile. Climb it, head uphill to climb another one and continue along the left edge of two fields, climbing more stiles. In the third field, bear right and head diagonally across it to a waymarked gate.

After going through it, bear left along the left edge of a field to a stile, climb it and keep ahead by a line of trees on the left which indicate the line of a former field boundary. Go through a hedge gap beside a redundant stile, continue along the right edge of the next field, climb a stile onto a lane and turn left. At a public footpath sign, turn right along a track and in front of a canal bridge, turn right through a gate and descend to the towpath of the Shropshire Union Canal. **D**

Turn sharp left, pass under the bridge and keep by the canal for 2 miles (3.2km) back to Audlem. On approaching a pub called the Shroppie Fly, bear left off the towpath to emerge onto a road by the Bridge Inn **E** and turn left to return to The Square. ●

Gawsworth Hall and North Rode

Start	Gawsworth, Harrington Arms
Distance	6½ miles (10.4km)
Approximate time	3 hours
Parking	Roadside parking by the Harrington Arms at Gawsworth
Refreshments	Pub at Gawsworth
Ordnance Survey maps	Explorer 268 (Wilmslow, Macclesfield & Congleton), Landranger 118 (Stoke-on-Trent & Macclesfield)

This walk reveals the Cheshire landscape at its most typical. It embraces lush, gently rolling pastures, woodland, parkland, black and white buildings, a stretch of canal and views of the Peak District hills on the horizon. The surroundings of Gawsworth Hall and church at the start are particularly attractive and the route is undemanding and easy to follow but be prepared for muddy conditions in places after wet weather.

Start by the Harrington Arms, walk along the lane signposted to Gawsworth Church and the lane bends first left and then right. The views to the right across the pool to the church and black and white, half-timbered hall are outstanding. The mainly Elizabethan hall was the home of the Fitton family, one of whom, Mary Fitton, is thought to be the Dark Lady of Shakespeare's sonnets. There are Fitton family tombs in the 15th-century church whose imposing Perpendicular tower rises to a height of 103 feet (31m).

Where the lane turns left, turn right along a tarmac drive **Ⓐ**. The drive curves left and where it bends right, keep ahead along a track. At a fork, climb a stile, continue along the right hand track and where it peters out, keep by the right edge of a field to a stile. Climb it, walk along the right edge of

fields, via kissing-gates, and finally continue along a track to a road.

Turn right and just before a railway bridge, turn right **Ⓑ** along Cowbrook Lane, signposted to Bosley. The lane bends left to cross a railway bridge. Keep along it as far as a canal bridge. In front of the bridge, bear left down steps, turn right to pass under the bridge **Ⓒ** and continue beside the Macclesfield Canal to bridge 54, by Bosley Locks. At the bridge keep ahead to go through a gate onto a road **Ⓓ**, turn right and where the road bends right immediately after a railway bridge, keep ahead and then climb a stile by a public footpath sign **Ⓔ**.

Walk along a tarmac track – tree-lined in places – through the parkland adjoining North Rode Manor, pass by the end of the lake and just before a gate and cattle-grid, bear left to a stile.

Climb it, keep ahead towards a farm, joining the left field edge, climb a stile and walk along a track to a public footpath sign  **F**. *Keep ahead along a tarmac track to see North Rode's Victorian church*; otherwise turn sharp right along a concrete drive. At a fork, keep along the left hand drive, go over a cattle-grid, pass to the left of a farm and climb the stile ahead.

Walk across a field, making for the left corner of the trees in front, where you pick up a track which curves right to a stile. Climb it, continue by the left edge of a field and climb another stile onto a lane. Turn right and at a T-junction, keep ahead over a stile **G**

and walk along the left edge of a field. Climb a stile, continue along a left field edge, climb two stiles in quick succession and keep ahead to climb another one. Walk along the left edge of the next two fields – there are fine views ahead of Gawsworth church tower – and in the third field, bear slightly right across it to a stile in the corner. Climb it, continue in the same diection across the next field, climb a stile in front of lakes, immediately climb another one and turn left beside a lake.

At a fork, take the left-hand path to continue beside the lake and at the

corner of it, keep ahead uphill and go through a hedge gap to a stile. Climb it, continue along the left edge of a succession of fields, climbing a series of stiles, and finally descend steps to a lane. Turn left to return to the start. ●

Gawsworth Church

Farndon and Churton

Start	Farndon
Distance	6½ miles (10.4km)
Approximate time	3 hours
Parking	Farndon Picnic Area
Refreshments	Pubs at Farndon, pub at Churton
Ordnance Survey maps	Explorer 257 (Crewe & Nantwich), Landranger 117 (Chester & Wrexham)

A pleasant walk across fields leads to Churton and from there the route continues along enclosed paths and through woodland to the River Dee, which here forms the border between England and Wales. The remainder of the route is mostly across meadows beside the winding river. The wide views across the surrounding flat terrain extend from Cheshire's sandstone ridge to the Clwydian hills of North Wales.

Farndon is an attractive village of stone and black-and-white, half-timbered cottages. The church, of medieval origin, was mainly rebuilt in the 17th century after being damaged in the Civil War.

🖉 Start at the picnic area by the 14th-century bridge over the River Dee and walk along a track away from the bridge. Just before reaching a boardwalk, bear left along a path which curves left and climb steps through woodland. At the top, turn first right and then left along a hedge-lined path to a lane and turn right to a road.

Cross over, keep ahead along a track (Walkers Lane), go through a kissing-gate and continue along the left edge of a field. Go through a kissing-gate, keep ahead across the next field and at a footpath post by a hedge corner, turn right **A** and continue along the left field hedge. At another hedge corner, keep straight ahead across the field and climb a stile onto a road. Turn left and at a public footpath sign to Churton and Coddington, turn right along a track.

Cheshire countryside near Farndon

Bridge over River Dee at Farndon

The Starling's Wood
KINGS MARSH
CP
Rowley Hill
Morrislake Bridge
Rowleyhill

| 0 | 200 | 400 | 600 | 800 METRES | 1 KILOMETRES |
| 0 | 200 | 400 | 600 YARDS | ½ | MILES |

at a meeting of several paths and tracks, turn sharp left **C** over a stile and walk across a field to a footbridge.

Cross it, walk along the left edge of the next field, climb a stile and continue along a tarmac track to a T-junction in the pleasant village of Churton. Turn left, at the next T-junction turn right to a road, turn right and almost immediately turn left beside the White Horse pub along Hob Lane **D**. Where the lane bends left, keep ahead along an enclosed path. Turn right at a T-junction, immediately turn left to continue along the path – later through woodland – and at a fork, take the left hand path to a footpath post.

Turn left, in the Farndon direction, along a tree-lined path beside the River Dee **E** and after climbing a stile, continue along the right edge of a field. Pass through a belt of trees, go through a gate, keep ahead and where the river bends right, go through a kissing-gate and keep ahead to emerge onto a track. Go through a kissing-gate, walk along the edge of a meadow and turn left through a gate to rejoin the river. Go through another gate, keep ahead along a track, turn right at a waymarked post – there are pools on the left – and at a public footpath sign, turn right up steps and walk along a fence-lined path to a kissing-gate. Go through, continue across riverside meadows, go through a kissing-gate and walk along an enclosed path to another kissing-gate.

After going through it, keep by the river and in the corner of the meadow, follow the edge to the left and turn right over a stile. Walk along a grassy path by the right edge of a field, go through a kissing-gate and now comes a most attractive finale as you continue by the Dee, going through a series of kissing-gates and finally going under an arch of Farndon Bridge to return to the starting point of the walk. ●

Pass to the left of farm buildings, go through two gates and continue along a concrete track.

Go through a gate into a field, bear left diagonally across it and in the corner, cross a plank footbridge and climb a stile. Walk along the left edge of the next field, go through a gate to a fingerpost and turn left, **B** in the Churton direction, along a broad, grassy, hedge-lined track (Marsh Lane). At the next footpath post, go through a gate, continue along a narrower enclosed track and where it ends, turn left along a narrow lane. Turn right at a junction and where the lane bends right

Disley and Lyme Park

Start	Disley, station car park
Distance	6½ miles (10.4km)
Approximate time	3 hours
Parking	Disley station
Refreshments	Pubs and cafés at Disley, café at Lyme Park
Ordnance Survey maps	Explorer OL1 (The Peak District – Dark Peak area), Landranger 109 (Manchester)

This highly scenic walk follows the first part of the Gritstone Trail along an old routeway into Lyme Park. Then comes a short circuit of the park, passing through attractive woodland and climbing across open moorland, before returning to Disley. The superb, extensive and contrasting views range from the built-up area of Greater Manchester to the bare moorlands of the Peak District and the route passes Lyme Hall, well worth a visit.

From the car park, begin by climbing the steps through woodland and pass beside a fence onto a lane. Keep ahead uphill and where the lane bends right, turn left along a tarmac track **Ⓐ**. At a fork, take the right hand enclosed track (Green Lane) and follow it gently uphill. There are fine views all round and the Cage in Lyme Park, a 16th-century tower built as a viewing platform for the hunt, is soon seen to the right. The track later narrows to a path and reaches a stile.

Climb it, keep ahead to ford a brook and the path bends right at a fence corner and continues to a gate **Ⓑ**. Go through, turn right downhill along an enclosed track, cross a bridge over a brook and head up to a gate by a lodge. Go through – here entering Lyme Park – and continue along the well-surfaced track ahead which curves gradually left and descends to the hall. The park, originally enclosed as a deer park from the surrounding Macclesfield Forest in

1346, comprises more than 1300 acres (525ha) of grassland, woodland and moorland.

Lyme Hall belonged to one family, the Leghs, for nearly 600 years but in 1946 Richard Legh, 3rd Lord Newton, gave both the hall and the park to the National Trust. The north front is part of the original 16th-century mansion built by Sir Piers Legh, as are the drawing room and long gallery. Over the next three centuries the house was enlarged and rebuilt on several occasions, notably in the early 18th century by the Italian architect Leoni, and again in the early 19th century by Lewis Wyatt. Leoni's main contribution was the elegant classical south front, the most popular view of the hall. Inside, the house is a treasure store of fine paintings, furniture and tapestries.

In front of the gates of the hall, turn right down steps **Ⓒ** to the car park, walk across it and continue along a broad tarmac track. At a fork, take the

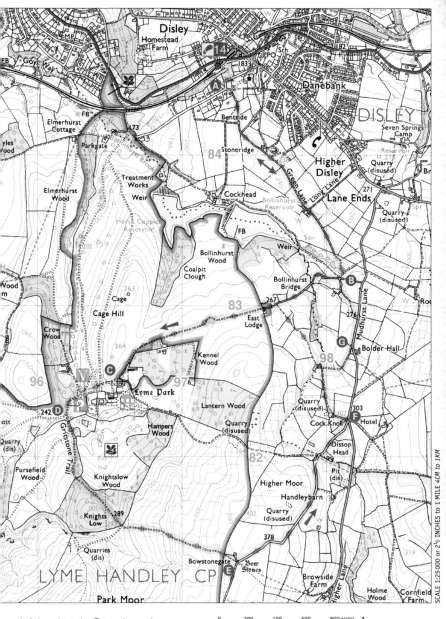

left hand track, **D** go through a kissing-gate and keep ahead uphill, later along the right edge of trees.

After climbing a ladder stile, the route continues steadily uphill through the delightful Knightslow Wood. To the left, the main façade of Lyme Hall can be seen through the trees. Climb a ladder stile on the far side of the wood, continue uphill across open moorland and climb another ladder stile to leave the park. Keep ahead and climb a stile onto a lane **E**. This is the highest point on the walk – around 1300 ft (396m) – and the views over the Peak District are magnificent, with Shutlingsloe's distinctive peak visible on the horizon.

Turn left along the lane, passing the Bow Stones, the middle sections of a group of Anglo-Saxon crosses. The lane winds downhill to a road 🇫. Immediately, turn left along a tarmac track to a farm, turn right through the farmyard and go through a gate by the corner of a barn. Head downhill across a field, climb a stile and continue along the left edge of the next field down to another stile. Do not climb it but turn right along a grassy path to a stile. Climb it, keep ahead, passing a barn, climb another stile, continue along a track and climb one more stile onto a road 🇬.

Turn left and at a public footpath sign, turn left down steps and go through a kissing-gate. Follow a path across an area planted by Macclesfield Borough Council as a Millennium Wood and after passing a redundant stile, bear left. Go through a kissing-gate and over a stile onto a track and turn right to a crossways 🇧. Keep ahead through a gate, here picking up the outward route, and retrace your steps to the start. ●

Lyme Park

Dunham Park and the Bridgewater Canal

Start	Oldfield Brow, Seamons Road car park, about 1 mile (1.6km) north west of Altrincham
Distance	6½ miles (10.4km)
Approximate time	3 hours
Parking	Seamons Road car park
Refreshments	Pub near start, pubs at Dunham Woodhouses, pub at Little Bollington, pub at Dunham Town, café at Dunham Massey Hall
Ordnance Survey maps	Explorers 268 (Wilmslow, Macclesfield & Congleton) and 276 (Bolton, Wigan & Warrington), Landranger 109(Manchester)

This route makes use of a disused railway track – part of the Trans-Pennine Trail – on the outward leg and the towpath of the Bridgewater Canal on the final stretch. In between you walk through part of the park surrounding the great house of Dunham Massey, a National Trust property. There are wide views across the pleasant countryside of the Bollin valley which lies between the Greater Manchester and Merseyside conurbations.

Start by turning left along a straight track, once a railway line between Altrincham and Warrington and now part of the Trans-Pennine Trail. Keep along it for 1½ miles (2.4km), passing under one bridge, to emerge onto a road (Station Road) **A**.

Turn left into Dunham Woodhouses and just after the road bends left in the village centre, turn right along an

Dunham Massey Hall

enclosed track (Meadow Lane). After crossing a bridge over the River Bollin, keep ahead over a stile and veer slightly left across a field to cross a footbridge over a brook. Bear slightly right and head uphill across a field, climb a stile on the brow and keep ahead across the next field to a fingerpost **B**. Turn left and continue across the field, making for a stile at a hedge corner.

Climb the stile, walk along the right edge of a field, climb two stiles in quick succession, follow a track across the next field and climb another stile on the far side. Continue along an enclosed track, climb a stile and keep ahead to pass under an aqueduct which carries the Bridgewater Canal over the track. The track emerges onto a lane in Little Bollington. Turn left and where the lane ends, keep ahead to cross a footbridge over the Bollin by a former mill. Continue along a tarmac track and where it bends left, pass beside a gate and walk along a straight, fence-lined path towards the buildings of Dunham Massey.

Climb a ladder stile to enter Dunham Park and keep ahead along a tarmac drive to a fork in front of the hall **C**. Dunham Massey Hall was built for the Earl of Warrington in the 18th century and remodelled in the early 20th century. It is noted for

Deer in Dunham Park

the richness of the interior and the fine collections of furniture, silver and paintings. There are colourful gardens and the surrounding deer park, laid out in the early 18th century, has some impressive avenues.

At the fork, take the right-hand drive and continue across the deer park, curving left to a lodge. Climb a ladder stile onto a road, **D** turn left and take the first lane on the right. At a public footpath sign, turn right over a stile, follow a path across a field and by a waymarked post on the far side, turn left to continue along the right field edge. Climb a stile onto a lane, turn right and at a public footpath sign, turn left over a stile and walk across a field

to a waymarked post on the far side. Turn left **E** along an enclosed path, pass beside a fence and continue to a road in Dunham Town which, despite its name, is only a hamlet.

Turn right, passing the small Victorian church, and immediately after crossing a canal bridge, **F** turn sharp right down a path and through a kissing-gate onto the towpath of the Bridgewater Canal. Turn left and keep beside the canal for 1 mile (1.6km) to Seamons Moss Bridge. Just before reaching it, turn left up steps to a road and turn left to return to the start. ●

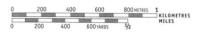

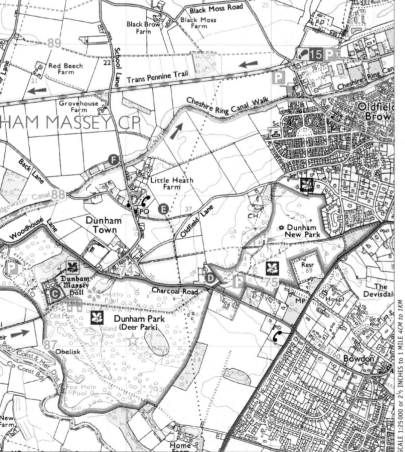

Beeston Castle and the Shropshire Union Canal

Start	Beeston Castle
Distance	6½ miles (10.5km)
Approximate time	3½ hours
Parking	Beeston Castle car park, free parking for walkers visiting the castle, otherwise a fee of £1 payable at the castle ticket office
Refreshments	Pub by Bate's Mill Bridge
Ordnance Survey maps	Explorers 257 (Crewe & Nantwich) and 267 (Northwich & Delamere Forest), Landranger 117 (Chester & Wrexham)

For most of the walk, there are striking views both of medieval Beeston Castle and Victorian Peckforton Castle, perched on neighbouring wooded hills overlooking the Cheshire plain. Much of the route is flat – across fields and along a canal towpath – but towards the end, a gentle climb through Pennsylvania Wood brings you onto the sandstone ridge followed by a walk through beautiful woodland along the ridge. After descending, the final stretch across fields brings the most spectacular views of all of Beeston Castle.

Beeston Castle has one of the most dramatic locations of any castle in the country, occupying the summit of a wooded hill which rises abruptly above the Cheshire plain. The mainly 13th-century fortress, one of the strongholds of the powerful earls of Chester, was built to protect the English border. In spite of its apparently impregnable position, it was successfully captured by a small Royalist force from its Parliamentary occupants in the Civil War.

Crowning the adjoining summit is Peckforton Castle, built in the middle of the 19th century as an almost perfect replica of a 12th-century fortress, a superb example of the desire of many wealthy Victorians to recreate medieval buildings and ideals.

🖊 Turn right out of the car park along a lane and at a Sandstone Trail sign, turn right through a kissing-gate, Ⓐ descend steps and follow a track across fields to a stile. Climb it, bear slightly left, head across a field to climb another stile and keep ahead across the next field towards a railway bridge. Climb a stile, pass under the bridge, climb another stile and continue towards a canal bridge. Cross a footbridge over a brook, head up to the bridge but before reaching it, turn right through a kissing-gate – here leaving the Sandstone Trail – and turn left to pass under the bridge Ⓑ. Walk along the towpath of the Shropshire Union Canal for just under 2 miles (3.2km), passing the Shady Oak Inn on the opposite bank. After crossing an aqueduct over the infant River Gowy – there is a fine view to the left here of Peckforton Castle – immediately turn left downhill,  by a fence on the left, turn left through a gate and descend steps beside the aqueduct. At the bottom, turn right along a tree-lined path – here joining the Eddisbury Way – to a stile. Climb it, keep ahead along the right edge of a field and just after

passing a gate in the hedge on the right, bear left diagonally across the field and turn left over a stile in the far corner.

Walk along an enclosed track which bends right to a T-junction, turn right and at a public footpath sign immediately after passing under a railway bridge, turn left up steps and climb a stile. Bear slightly right across a field, making for the left side of a tree-fringed pool, climb a stile and continue

Beeston Castle

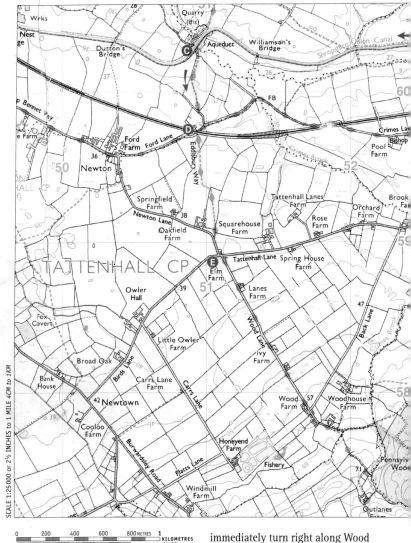

SCALE 1:25 000 or 2½ INCHES to 1 MILE 4CM to 1KM

0 200 400 600 800 METRES 1 KILOMETRES
0 200 400 600 YARDS ½ MILES

in the same direction across the next field to a stile.

Climb it, turn left along a fence-lined track and where it bends right, keep ahead over a stile. Bear right diagonally across a field, climb a stile and almost immediately turn left over a footbridge. Turn right along the right edge of a field, cross a footbridge in the corner, keep along the right edge of the next field and look out for where you turn right over a stile onto a lane. Turn left to a T-junction, turn left and almost

immediately turn right along Wood Lane ⒠. Where the lane bends left, continue along first a tarmac track and then a cobbled track and where the track bends left to a farm, keep ahead over a stone stile.

Walk across a field towards a waymarked stile but before reaching it, turn left over a stile to the left of a gate and turn right along the right edge of a field. Cross a footbridge over a brook and bear right to climb a stile on the edge of Pennsylvania Wood. Follow a path uphill along the left inside edge of the trees and after going through a gate, continue through the wood. Look out

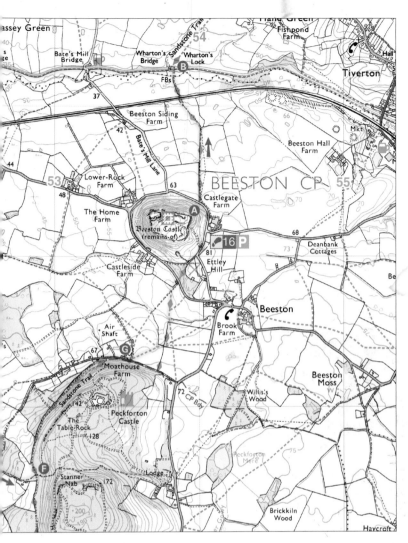

for where a waymarked post directs you to turn left and cross a plank footbridge to reach a track. Cross it, take the path ahead, signposted to Peckforton and Beeston Moss, and continue uphill along the right inside edge of the wood. Go through a fence gap, keep ahead and on emerging from the trees, bear left along a track.

At a crossways turn left **F**, in the Beeston Castle direction, along a track to rejoin the Sandstone Trail. The track continues through delightful woodland below Peckforton Castle, gradually descending to a lane. Turn right and at a public footpath sign, bear left over a stile **G** and follow a path diagonally across a field to a stile in the far corner. From now on there are superb views of Beeston Castle. Climb the stile, turn left along a track by the left edge of a field, climb another stile and keep ahead through a belt of trees to cross a footbridge.

Ascend steps, climb a stile, continue across a field, climb another stile on the far side and keep ahead to a lane. Cross over, climb a stile and head uphill through woodland, later keeping along the top inside edge of the trees. Continue along an enclosed path to a lane and turn left to return to the start. ●

Caldy Hill, Thurstaston and the Wirral Way

Start	Wirral Way, Thurstaston Centre, signposted from A540 at Thurstaston
Distance	7 miles (11.2km)
Approximate time	3½ hours
Parking	Thurstaston Centre
Refreshments	Café at start, pub at Thurstaston
Ordnance Survey maps	Explorer 266 (Wirral & Chester), Landranger 108 (Liverpool)

The opening and closing stretches are along the Wirral Way beside the Dee estuary. Much of the remainder of the route is through the extensive woodlands and across the heathlands of the adjacent Caldy Hill, Stapledon Wood and Thurstaston Common. There are a series of superb viewpoints but the finest is the summit of Thurstaston Hill which, despite its modest height, 255 ft (78m), offers magnificent views over both the Dee and Mersey estuaries.

Wirral Country Park Visitor Centre at Thurstaston is situated on a grassy clifftop above the Dee estuary and there are fine views across the water to the hills of North Wales. The Wirral Way, a footpath and cycleway, uses the track of a former railway which ran along the western side of the Wirral.

From the car park descend steps to the Wirral Way, turn right to pass between the platforms of the former Thurstaston station and go under a bridge. Continue along the track – on this stretch it is a 'dual carriageway' with a parallel footpath and cycleway – and just after the two tracks join, you reach a road **A**. Turn right, at a fork take the left hand road which curves right to a T-junction and turn left. Look out for a public footpath sign and turn right onto an enclosed path which

bends right and heads up to a road. Turn left and where the road bends right, turn left, at a footpath post, along a path for a brief detour through woodland to a viewpoint on the slopes of Caldy Hill. Go through a gap in a wall, take the right hand path at a fork, keep ahead at all path junctions and head up to a clearing for a superb view overlooking the Dee estuary **B**.

Retrace your steps to the road and turn left. At a fork take the right hand road (Kings Drive) and where it ends, keep ahead beside a barrier, at a public bridleway sign, and follow a path through the delightful Stapledon Wood. After passing beside another barrier, keep ahead to a road, turn right and take the first road on the left (Grange Cross Lane). At a public footpath sign to Frankby, turn right over a stile **C** and

SCALE 1:27777 or about 2¼ INCHES to 1 MILE 3.6CM to 1KM

| 0 | 200 | 400 | 600 | 800 METRES | 1 |
| 0 | 200 | 400 | 600 YARDS | ½ | KILOMETRES MILES |

walk along an enclosed path which bears left to another stile.

Climb it, head across a field to join and keep beside its left edge and in the corner, climb a stone stile onto a track. Follow the track around first a right bend and then a left bend to reach a road and turn right. At a public footpath sign to Thurstaston, turn left along a tree-lined track **D** to enter Royden Park. This former Victorian estate, together with the adjoining Thurstaston Common, comprise a large public access area of woodland, heathland and parkland. On reaching a tarmac track, Royden Park Visitor Centre is ahead but the route continues to the right. Look out for where a sign to Thurstaston Common directs you to turn left onto a path which continues by the left inside edge of woodland.

Turn right in front of a short stretch of wall and follow the path to the left to continue across the heathland and woodland of the common to a kissing-gate. Go through, keep ahead and at a fork shortly after passing a farm on the left, take the right hand narrower path and go through a kissing-gate onto a lane.

Bear right and go up three steps to climb the short distance to the triangulation pillar and viewfinder on the summit of Thurstaston Hill . The views from here are tremendous, taking in the buildings of Liverpool, the Wirral and the hills of North Wales. In clear conditions they extend to the Great Orme and the Snowdonia range.

Retrace your steps to the bottom of the hill, turn sharp right along a track and go through a kissing-gate onto a road. Bear left into Thurstaston, at a crossroads turn right along Station Road and at a T-junction, turn left along a lane,  passing to the left of the red sandstone Victorian church. In the churchyard is the early 19th-century tower of its predecessor. Where the lane bends left, keep ahead along a track at a public footpath sign to Heswall to a stile. Climb it, continue along an enclosed path, negotiating a kissing-gate and several stiles, and after reaching a footpath post in a belt of trees, turn right, in the Wirral Way direction . The path heads gently downhill through the lovely wooded dell of the Dungeon to a waymarked post.

Turn left to descend steps, turn right, head up an embankment and turn right to rejoin the Wirral Way . In front of gates, bear left along a path which bends left to a T-junction, turn right and follow a track back to the start. ●

Dee estuary near Thurstaston

Trent and Mersey Canal and Great Budworth

Start	Marbury Country Park
Distance	7 miles (11.2km)
Approximate time	3½ hours
Parking	Marbury Country Park
Refreshments	Pub at Anderton, pub at Marston, pub at Great Budworth
Ordnance Survey maps	Explorer 267 (Northwich & Delamere Forest), Landranger 118 (Stoke-on-Trent & Macclesfield)

There is plenty of historic interest on this walk as it starts at a former country estate and passes a unique monument to the Industrial Revolution and a medieval church. The route falls into three distinct segments. First comes a walk across fields to the canal at Anderton. This is followed by a 2½-mile (4-km) stretch beside the Trent and Mersey Canal, passing the Anderton Boat Lift. More field walking leads first to the attractive village of Great Budworth and then back to the start. On the final stretch there are fine views over Budworth Mere.

Marbury Country Park, created in 1975, occupies the grounds of the former estate of the Marbury family, who were involved in the early salt industry of Northwich. After being requisitioned in the Second World War, the house was demolished in 1969.

Facing towards Budworth Mere, take the path in the right hand (north east) corner of the car park, passing beside a metal barrier to a country park information board. Keep ahead to go through a gate and turn left along a broad tarmac track. Follow it first around a right bend, in the Budworth Mere direction, then around a left bend, in the Bird Hide direction, and keep ahead, passing beside a barrier, to a road. Turn right and at a public footpath sign, turn left **A** over a stile and walk

along the right edge of a field to another stile. Climb it, keep ahead through trees, cross a footbridge over a stream and climb a stile to exit from the trees.

Walk across the next two fields, climbing two stiles, to emerge onto a lane. Climb the stile opposite, walk across a field, go througn a wide gap and bear left along the left edge of the next field above a ditch. Climb a stile and continue along the right edge of fields, climbing two more stiles, and climb a final stile onto a road **B**. Turn left into Anderton and at a T-junction, turn sharp right over a canal bridge. Turn right through a hedge gap onto the towpath and turn right again **C** to pass under the bridge.

Walk along the towpath of the Trent and Mersey Canal to the Anderton Boat

Lift, an outstanding example of Victorian engineering. It was built in 1875 in order to transfer boats up or down the 50 ft (15m) from the River Weaver to the canal and was the first of its kind in the world. There is a visitor centre and a nature park reclaimed from industrial wasteland. On the other side of the river is a huge ICI complex. A bridge over the canal leads to the pub on the opposite bank.

Continue by the canal – soon the woodlands of Marbury Country Park are seen over to the left – as far as bridge 193 and turn right in front of it up to a road **D**. A pub and the entrance to the Lion Salt Works Museum are to the right. The route continues to the left over the bridge and between flashes, the latter caused by subsidence. At a public footpath sign, turn left **E** along a tarmac track and where it ends at a farm, keep ahead along a narrow enclosed path to a stile.

Climb it, continue along the right edge of a field, turn right over another stile and follow a track diagonally across the next field. On the far side where the track curves left, keep ahead over a stile, walk along the left edge of a field and climb a stile in the corner. Cross a track, climb the stile opposite and walk along the right edge of fields, heading downhill to climb a stile onto a road **F**.

Anderton Boat Lift

Turn left and at a public footpath sign, turn right over a stile and head uphill along the left edge of a field, curving right to continue along the edge to a stile. After climbing it, keep ahead along a hedge-lined track and

later a tarmac track towards Great Budworth Church, turn left and pass in front of the church to the village centre Ⓖ. With its impressive 15th-century church and half-timbered cottages, Great Budworth is exceptionally attractive.

Turn left down High Street to a crossroads and keep ahead, in the Comberbach and Runcorn direction. After ½ mile (800m), turn left, Ⓗ at a public footpath sign, along a path which leads down through trees and pass beside a fence gap on the far side of the wood. Keep ahead across a field and later continue along its right edge to a stile. From here there are fine views to the left over Budworth Mere. Climb the stile, keep ahead to cross a footbridge over a brook and continue along the right edge of a field to another stile.

Climb it, walk across the next field and go through a kissing-gate onto a road. Turn left and after passing a public footpath sign on the right, you pick up the outward route and retrace your steps to the start. ●

Wybunbury

Start	Wybunbury
Distance	7½ miles (12km)
Approximate time	3½ hours
Parking	Roadside parking at Wybunbury
Refreshments	Pubs at Wybunbury, cafés at Dagfields Craft Centre
Ordnance Survey maps	Explorer 257 (Crewe & Nantwich), Landranger 118 (Stoke-on-Trent & Macclesfield)

From the hilltop village of Wybunbury, the route follows tracks, field paths and lanes across the undulating country of south Cheshire to the south, east and north of the village. Towards the end it passes the edge of Wybunbury Moss, a National Nature Reserve. For much of the way, Wybunbury's imposing church tower is in sight. There are more than 30 stiles to climb.

The tall, 15th-century church tower at Wybunbury stands on its own; unstable ground caused the church to be rebuilt several times throughout its history and it was finally abandoned and demolished in the 1970s. A modern church building is nearby.

🖉 The walk starts by the Swan Inn. Facing the church tower, walk down the hill to the right of it and just after crossing a bridge over Wybunbury Brook, turn right, at a public footpath sign, along a tarmac track. By a cattle-grid, turn left along the left edge of a field and look out for where you turn left up steps to climb a stile.

Bear right, head across to climb another stile and turn left along the left edge of a field. Follow the edge to the right and continue along a track to the A51. Turn right, at a public footpath sign turn left Ⓐ over a stile, walk across a field to a fence corner and then bear right and continue across the field to cross a footbridge in the far right corner. Keep along a right field edge and at a fence corner, veer slightly right

and head across to a stile. Climb it, turn right along the right edge of the next field and where the edge bends right, keep straight ahead and climb a stile on the far side.

Continue across the next field, climb a stile, cross a footbridge and then keep ahead across a succession of fields and over a series of stiles, finally turning left along a tarmac track. About 100 yds (91m) before reaching a road, turn right onto a narrow path and walk across a field to a stile. Climb it, keep ahead to a track – there is a pool on the left – and follow the track around a number of bends to a road. Dagfields Craft Centre (which has cafés) is to the left; the route continues to the right. Take the first lane on the left (Lodge Lane) Ⓑ and follow it around a right bend to a T-junction. Turn left and after ¼ mile (400m), turn left, at a public footpath sign, to join the South Cheshire Way Ⓒ.

Walk along the right edge of a field, follow the edge to the left to continue by Birchenhill Wood on the right, head down into a dip and after climbing a

stile, veer slightly left across the corner of the field and cross a footbridge. Continue uphill along the right edge of a young plantation, climb a stile, keep along the right field edge and turn right over a stile at a wall corner. Walk across a field, climb another stile and turn left along a track to the A51. *Cross carefully – this is a very busy road* – turn left along the verge, turn right into the drive to Lea Forge Farm **D** but immediately bear right through a fence gap, at a public bridleway sign, and continue along a path parallel to the drive.

Near Wybunbury

Continue past it, keeping to the right of a pool, to a hedge corner and keep along the right field edge. After curving left, turn right over a stile in the field corner, immediately turn left over another one and walk along a path by the side of a house to a road. Turn right, follow the road around a left bend – here leaving the South Cheshire Way. At a public footpath sign, turn left over a stile **F** to join the Crewe and Nantwich Circular Walk.

Walk along a narrow enclosed path to a stile, climb it and continue along the right edge of a succession of fields, climbing a series of stiles. At a fence corner, follow the field edge to the right, climb a stile and continue along the right edge of more fields, climbing more stiles. At the corner of a hedge, keep straight across the field to a stile, climb it, walk along the right edge of the next field and in the corner, turn left to continue along the edge to a fence corner. Bear right and keep along the left edge of a pool to a stile, climb it and bear left across a field in the direction of Wybunbury Church tower.

Climb a stile and continue in the same direction across the next field. Climb another stile on the right-hand side and keep ahead by the left edge of Wybunbury Moss – the path is likely to be boggy and there is a boardwalk. Wybunbury Moss, a National Nature Reserve, is a rare and valuable example of a floating bog i.e. peat floating on water. Cross a footbridge, head uphill towards the church and go through a kissing-gate into the churchyard. Go through another gate by the tower and turn right to return to the start. ●

Turn left through a gate onto the drive, turn right to cross a bridge over a brook, head uphill and at a public bridleway sign, go through a gate and continue uphill along an enclosed path. At a footpath post, turn right up to a stile, climb it and turn left along the left edge of a field. The next part of the route is an undulating one. Climb a stile, keep along the left edge of a field, climb another stile and continue along the right edge of the next field towards a farm. After climbing the next stile, keep ahead between farm buildings – there are several gates – and turn left by a barn along a concrete drive which curves right to a road **E**. Turn left, at a public footpath sign turn right through a gate, walk across a field over a low brow and descend to a stile.

Climb it, turn right along the right edge of a field, climb a stile in the corner and turn left to head gently uphill along a left field edge to a stile. Climb it, cross a track, climb the stile opposite and walk across a field, making for the right hand one of a line of telegraph poles (waymarked).

Wirral Way, Parkgate and the Dee estuary

Start	Wirral Way, Hadlow Road Station, signposted from B5133 at Willaston
Distance	8 miles (12.9km)
Approximate time	4 hours
Parking	Hadlow Road Station
Refreshments	Pubs and cafés at Parkgate, pub at Little Neston, pub at Ness
Ordnance Survey maps	Explorer 266 (Wirral & Chester), Landranger 117 (Chester & Wrexham)

Much of the route is along the Wirral Way, a former railway track, which provides easy and pleasant walking along tree-lined embankments and through deep cuttings. In complete contrast, the middle stretch, between Parkgate and Little Neston, takes you along the edge of the extensive marshes bordering the Dee estuary, from where there are superb views looking across to the hills of North Wales.

Wirral Country Park is based around the Wirral Way, a disused railway track. Most of the track was converted into a footpath and bridleway after the railway closed down in the 1960s. The railway, built in 1865, ran along the western side of the Wirral and the station at Hadlow Road has been preserved as it was in 1952, with the original waiting room, ticket office and signal box.

🖉 Begin by walking along the platform of the former station, go through a gate, cross the road and take the track opposite to join the Wirral Way. Follow it for the next 2 miles (3.2km) – along the top of tree-lined embankments and later through a deep sandstone cutting – to reach a road in Neston **Ⓐ**. Here the track has been obliterated and the route continues

along Station Road. Where the road ends, pass under a railway bridge and keep ahead to regain the disused railway track.

Follow it for another ³⁄₄ mile (1.2km), eventually passing beside a gate and continuing along a tarmac track to a road in Parkgate. Turn left to a T-junction in front of the Dee estuary **Ⓑ**. The village centre, which has a pleasantly old fashioned and rather abandoned air about it, is to the right. In the 18th century, Parkgate was an important port with a flourishing passenger trade across the estuary to Wales and with Ireland. But the relentless silting up of the Dee, which had earlier destroyed Chester as a port, continued and Parkgate's prosperity declined. It enjoyed a brief revival in the 19th century as a holiday resort and

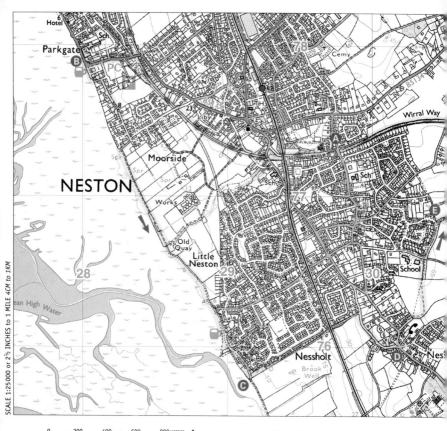

SCALE 1:25 000 or 2½ INCHES to 1 MILE 4CM to 1KM

The Parade, lined with 17th- to 19th-century buildings, still retains something of the atmosphere of a fashionable promenade.

At the T-junction the route continues to the left. Where the road peters out, keep ahead along a paved path above the marshes and the path bends left to emerge onto a tarmac drive. Turn right, pass beside a barrier to continue along a fence-lined path, pass beside another barrier and keep ahead along Manorial Road South. At a junction, turn right beside a barrier and walk along a grassy enclosed path which bends left to continue beside the marshes of the estuary again. There are fine views across the estuary to the hills of North Wales and the walls and towers of Flint Castle can be seen. Initially this part of the walk is likely to be muddy at times but later a paved path leads to a stile.

Climb it, veer slightly left to continue along the top of a low embankment, cross a footbridge over a stream and keep ahead to climb a stone stile at Old Quay. The broken walls here are among a number of remains of former wharves along this part of the estuary. Continue at first along a path by the edge of the marshes and as you join a track, the coal tip to the left is a reminder that there was once a colliery here. Pass in front of houses to reach the Harp Inn, continue past the pub and at a fence corner just beyond the last of the houses on the left, turn left along a tarmac path **Ⓒ**.

At a T-junction, turn right to continue along a tarmac path which bends left to keep by garden fences. Pass beside a barrier, keep ahead and at the next T-junction, turn right and then

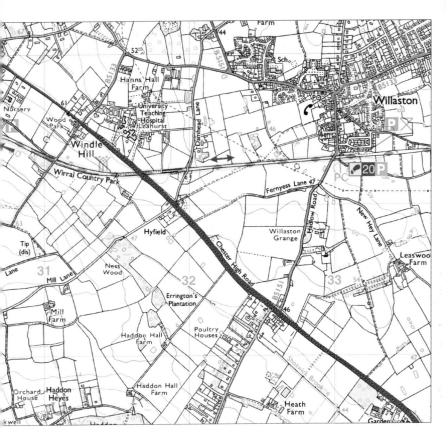

almost immediately turn left over a stile. Walk along an enclosed path and after passing under a railway bridge, the route continues along an ascending track to a lane. Turn right and the lane curves left to a crossroads in Ness **D**.

Turn left and at a left bend, turn right along an enclosed tarmac track (Cumbers Lane). Where the track bends left, keep ahead along an enclosed path. After going up two steps, the way continues across a field, following a path which curves left to a stile on the far side. Climb it, walk along the left edge of a playing field to a lane and keep ahead along Gorstons Lane. Just before a junction, turn right, **E** at a public bridleway sign,

along an enclosed path. The path bends left and gently descends to a disused railway bridge.

Just before the bridge, turn left over a stile and head up an embankment to rejoin the Wirral Way. Turn right and retrace your steps to the start. ●

Hadlow Road Station

Timbersbrook and The Cloud

Start	Timbersbrook Picnic Area, about 2 miles (3.2km) to the east of Congleton
Distance	6 miles (9.6km) Two shorter options of 4 miles (6.4km) and 2½ miles (4km)
Approximate time	3 hours (2 hours and 1½ hours for the two shorter walks)
Parking	Timbersbrook Picnic Area
Refreshments	None
Ordnance Survey maps	Explorer 268 (Wilmslow, Macclesfield & Congleton), Landranger 118 (Stoke-on-Trent & Macclesfield)

A walk across fields and beside the Macclesfield Canal is followed by a steady and relatively easy climb to the summit of The Cloud, 1125 ft (343m) high and a magnificent viewpoint. After the descent the route passes by a prehistoric burial chamber. There are a series of fine and contrasting views, both across the Cheshire plain and the hills and moors of the Peak District. As it is almost a figure-of-eight, the route can be divided into two shorter walks: the 4-mile (6.4-km) walk is basically an ascent of The Cloud; the 2¹⁄₂-mile (4-km) one omits The Cloud but includes the canal.

Timbersbrook is so green and quiet nowadays that it is almost impossible to envisage it as a noisy industrial area, the site of the Silver Springs Bleaching and Dyeing Company works. There is an information board in the car park.

📷 Begin by turning right out of the car park along a lane. Just after crossing a brook, turn left Ⓐ along a track, at a public footpath sign, joining both the Gritstone Trail and the Staffordshire Way.

If doing the 4-mile (6.4-km) walk, continue along the lane and rejoin the full walk at point Ⓓ.

After passing in front of a house, keep ahead along a path beside a factory building and descend steps to cross a footbridge over Timbers Brook. Ascend steps to climb a stile, bear slightly left across a field, climb a stile and keep ahead across the next field, heading down into a dip and up again to another stile. Climb it, turn right along the right edge of a field and at a Gritstone Trail post, turn left and continue across the field, by a line of trees on the right. Climb a stile, head in the same direction across the next field towards a farm, keep to the right of the farm buildings and on the far side of the field, climb two stiles in quick succession. Turn left along a path which curves right and climb a stone stile onto a lane **B**.

Turn right, at a public footpath sign turn left along a concrete track, go through a gate and continue along an enclosed track. Climb a stone stile, walk along the right edge of a field and in the corner, turn right over a stile. Keep along the left edge of the next field,

parallel to a disused railway track on the left, continue along the left edge of the next two fields, finally climbing a stile and descending steps to the Macclesfield Canal.

Turn right beside it and after going through a gate, turn left to cross a canal bridge. Immediately turn left through a gate, go down steps and turn sharp left to pass under the bridge. Continue beside the canal and just before the next bridge (no 71), turn left up to a T-junction **C**. Turn right to cross the bridge and keep ahead along a path through trees to enter a field. Ahead are superb views of The Cloud. Continue across the undulating field, bearing slightly right and making for the far right corner. Climb a stile, keep ahead along a track and climb another stile onto a lane **D**.

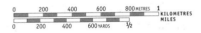

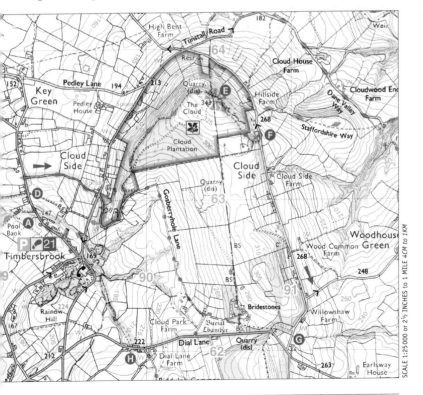

SCALE 1:25 000 or 2½ INCHES to 1 MILE 4CM to 1KM

View from The Cloud

Turn right to return to the start if doing the 2½-mile (4-km) walk.

For the full walk, turn left and at a public footpath sign, turn right beside a gate, here rejoining the Gritstone Trail and Staffordshire Way, and head gently uphill along a tree-lined track (Acorn Lane). The track later heads more steeply uphill to a road. Cross over, continue along the uphill track ahead (Gosberryhole Lane) through trees and follow it around a left bend to a fork. Take the left hand rocky path, passing a National Trust sign 'The Cloud', to a T-junction and turn left. Continue uphill, curving right, pass beside a fence, at a Gritstone Trail waymark, and follow the direction of the waymark – there are several paths here – uphill along a track to emerge from the trees onto heathery moorland.

Follow the winding path uphill through the heather to the triangulation pillar on the summit **E**. This magnificent and contrasting all-round viewpoint includes the hills and moors of the eastern Peak District, the Cheshire plain, Congleton, Macclesfield and Jodrell Bank. Beyond the summit, the path bears right to continue along the edge, descending gently. After passing through a fence gap, walk along an enclosed path, descend steps to a T-junction and turn left along a track which bends right to a lane **F**.

Turn right and after ¾ mile (1.2km), take the first lane on the right **G** which curves left to a road. Turn right and a short detour along a tarmac track to the right brings you to the prehistoric burial chamber of the Bridestones. Continue along the road to a public footpath sign and turn right **H** through a gate. Climb the stile ahead, bear gradually left across a field, making for the far left corner, keep ahead to pass between redundant gateposts and continue through a shallow valley by Timbers Brook on the left. Bear right away from the brook up to a stile, climb it and keep ahead by the left edge of a field above the sloping wooded valley of the brook.

Where the field ends on a narrow ridge, turn left downhill and cross a footbridge over the brook. Head uphill to climb a stone stile, turn right along a lane and keep ahead at a crossroads to the start. ●

Barthomley, Englesea-brook and Weston

Start	Barthomley
Distance	8 miles (12.9km)
Approximate time	4 hours
Parking	Roadside parking by the church and pub at Barthomley or village hall car park
Refreshments	Pub at Barthomley, pub at Weston
Ordnance Survey maps	Explorer 257 (Crewe & Nantwich), Landranger 118 (Stoke-on-Trent & Macclesfield)

The walk explores the pleasant and gently undulating countryside of south Cheshire and both Barthomley and Englesea-brook are particularly attractive and interesting villages. There are extensive views but be prepared for some muddy paths in places. Also note that there are around 50 stiles to climb, some of which require a reasonable degree of agility.

Barthomley is a pretty village with black-and-white houses and cottages and a thatched pub presided over by a fine 15th-century church.

🖉 Start by the White Lion and take the road signposted to Weston. Almost immediately turn left along a tarmac track, passing to the right of the church, walk through the village hall car park and keep ahead along an enclosed path to a stile.

Climb it, immediately turn left to climb another and head across a field to a stile on the far side. After climbing that one, keep ahead across the next two fields, climbing two more stiles, walk along the left edge of the next field, go up steps and over a stile and turn right to keep parallel to the right edge of a field.

Climb a stile, bear slightly left across a sloping field to climb a stile in trees, turn right and the path descends to keep along the right edge of a pool. Continue along a track above a brook on the right towards a farm, pass to the left of the farm buildings and keep ahead along an enclosed track. The track bends right and after passing to the right of another farm, continue along a tarmac track to a T-junction **Ⓐ**. Turn right along a lane, turn left over a stile, at a public footpath sign, and take a path which keeps along the edge of a garden to a stile. Climb it, continue across the next two fields, via two more stiles, and in the third field, keep ahead to a hedge corner and then bear left along its left edge to climb a stile. Bear right diagonally across a field, climb a stile and continue across two more fields, finally climbing a stile onto a lane.

Turn right into Englesea-brook, passing the chapel, built in 1828. In the early 19th century, the village was a centre for the radical Primitive

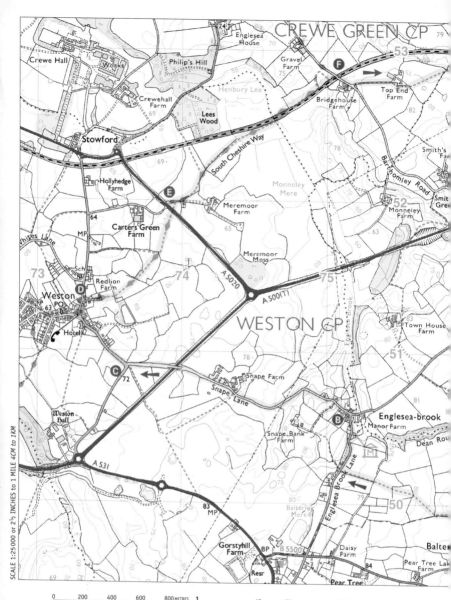

SCALE 1:25 000 or 2½ INCHES to 1 MILE 4CM to 1KM

Methodist movement and next to the chapel is a Primitive Methodism heritage centre. At a T-junction **B** turn left along Snape Lane and after 1¼ miles (2km), turn right, **C** at another T-junction, along a road into Weston. Soon after passing the White Lion and brick Victorian church, turn right, **D** at a South Cheshire Way sign, along a lane which soon becomes a track. Climb a

stile, walk across a field, cross a footbridge over a brook and keep ahead across the next field to climb a stile on the far side. Head gently uphill across the next field to a stile.

The next stile can be seen straight ahead but at the time of writing, sand extracting operations have obliterated the path and created a chasm and therefore a diversion (well-signposted) has to be made to reach it. After following the diversion and climbing the stile, head gently downhill across a

footbridge, then climb a stile and keep ahead, between wire fences and below a railway embankment, to a stile. After climbing it, turn left to climb another one, go under a railway bridge and turn right to cross a footbridge over a brook. Continue below the railway embankment, climb a stile and walk along the right edge of a field to climb another stile. Keep ahead along the edge of a young plantation, climb a stile onto a lane and turn right to cross a railway bridge **F**.

At a public footpath sign, turn left along the track to Top End Farm and by the farm buildings, look out for where you turn right over a stile. Turn left along the left edge of a field, following the yellow waymarks, turn left over a stile, keep ahead across the next field and climb a stile in the far right corner. Bear right across a field, making for a half-hidden stile in a dip, and after climbing it, walk across a field to the next stile. Climb it, keep ahead and go through a hedge gap onto a lane at a bend **G**.

Turn right and at a public footpath sign, turn left over a stile **H** and walk along the right edge of a field to climb another stile. Continue along the right edge of fields, climbing more stiles, and finally keep ahead along an enclosed track which bends left to a stile. Climb it and where the track bends left, turn right over a stile and descend steps to the busy A500 **J**. Cross carefully, ascend steps, climb a stile and turn left along the left edge of a field. After climbing the next stile, bear right across a field in the direction of Barthomley Church tower, climb a stile and head diagonally across the next field.

Climb a stile in the corner, keep ahead to climb another one and walk along an enclosed path which emerges onto a track. Bear left to a road and turn right to return to the start. ●

field and climb a stile onto the A5020 **E**. Cross carefully, climb the stile opposite, bear slightly left across the corner of a field and climb a stile onto a tarmac track. Turn right but almost immediately bear left, at a South Cheshire Way sign, along an enclosed path to a stile. Climb it, head across a field corner and continue along the right edge of the field.

Look out for where you turn right over a stile, turn left to keep along the left edge of the next field, cross a

Above Helsby and Frodsham

Start	Helsby Quarry Woodland Park on Helsby Hill
Distance	7 miles (11.2km)
Approximate time	3½ hours
Parking	Helsby Quarry Woodland Park
Refreshments	Pub at point **F**
Ordnance Survey maps	Explorer 267 (Northwich & Delamere Forest), Landranger 117 (Chester & Wrexham)

The sandstone ridge which runs north to south across Cheshire ends abruptly at steep wooded cliffs that plunge down to the adjacent towns of Helsby and Frodsham. These cliffs overlook the River Mersey and the industries of Merseyside and, from the higher points of the walk, there are a series of dramatic views over the estuary. There is also much attractive and enjoyable woodland walking. This is quite an energetic route, with a lot of ascents and descents – some of them steep – and some fairly difficult walking in places along rocky, winding and uneven paths across the thickly-wooded cliffsides.

Begin by walking up Hill Road South (almost opposite the car park) and where the road ends, keep ahead beside a fence to enter woodland. There is a National Trust sign 'Helsby Hill' here. The path curves right, continues uphill and at a fork, take the right hand path which passes between rock faces. Pass through a fence gap and keep ahead along a track beside a pool on the left.

After passing beside a gate, bear right along a narrow lane which heads downhill and curves left. At a public footpath sign to Tarvin Road and Commonside, turn right through a gate and walk along the left edge of a field to a kissing-gate. After going through that, turn left along the left edge of a field, climb a stile and head gently

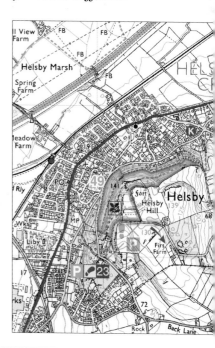

downhill along the left edge of the next field. The path bends right and continues along the field edge down to a stile. Turn left over it and walk along an enclosed path to a road **A**.

Turn left and at a public footpath sign, turn right through a kissing-gate and walk along the right edge of a field. Look out for where you turn right through a kissing-gate, cross a footbridge and turn left to continue along the left edge of a field. After climbing a stile, keep ahead along a track and go through a kissing-gate onto a lane. Turn left, at a T-junction turn right and at a public footpath sign to Woodhouse Hill and Frodsham, bear left along a tree-lined track **B**. The track continues through a steep-sided wooded valley, rising gently to a T-junction **C**.

Turn right, continue uphill through woodland – there are steps in places – and keep ahead along an enclosed path. Go through a gate, continue along a track to a road and turn left. At a public footpath sign, turn left **D** over a stile in a hedge and walk across a field, making for the corner of trees. Climb a stile, cross a track, climb the stile opposite and continue along an enclosed path. After climbing the next stile, walk along the left edge of a field to emerge onto a road.

Turn left and at a public footpath sign to Belle Monte and Frodsham, turn

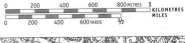

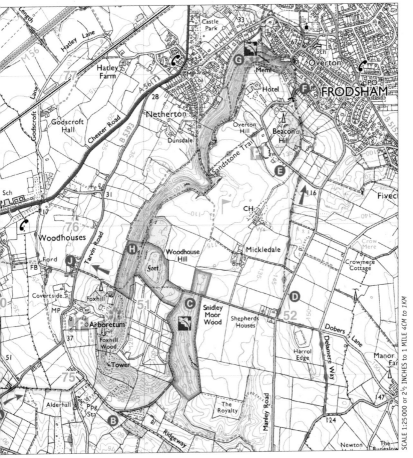

right along an enclosed track **E**. Where the track curves left to a cottage, continue along a grassy path to a gate. Go through, keep ahead to cross a tarmac track and continue along a path through trees. The path heads down across the hillside to a road. Turn right downhill and where the road bends right, turn left in front of the Belle Monte Hotel **F**.

Almost immediately bear right onto a wooded path and at a fork, take the left-hand upper path, signposted 'Mersey View via Lady's Walk'. Continue through woodland and at the next fork, take the left hand upper path again. At a Sandstone Trail post, turn left and head steeply uphill to the war memorial and viewpoint **G**. At 443 ft (135m), the views over Merseyside and the estuary are spectacular. From here, keep ahead along a path, by a wire fence on the left – through trees, gorse and bracken – and at a fork, take the right hand lower path, continuing across the hillside and following the regular Sandstone Trail waymarks.

On reaching a fingerpost, turn right, in the Woodhouse Hill direction, and

continue across the top of the wooded cliff. Soon you descend a flight of steps and turn right at the bottom. Keep following the Sandstone Trail waymarks and look out for where one of these directs you to turn right for a brief rock scramble before continuing along the cliff top. Over to the left is a golf course. By a bench and a view of Helsby Hill, the Sandstone Trail turns left but you keep ahead through the trees.

At a footpath post, bear right, **H** in the Helsby direction, and descend steeply – this is one of the most difficult parts of the walk – to emerge onto a tarmac track at the bottom, via a kissing-gate. Keep ahead, in the Tarvin Road direction, to a road, turn left and almost immediately, turn right **J** along a tarmac track (Chestnut Lane). Cross a footbridge over a brook, go up steps, climb a stile and walk across a field to climb another one. Keep ahead along a narrow enclosed path to climb a stile, continue across a field, climb another stile, walk along an enclosed path and go through a gate onto a road. Turn right, turn left at a crossroads and at a public footpath sign to Helsby Hill, turn left along a narrow enclosed path **K**.

View from Helsby Hill

Head uphill through woodland and the path bends right to a stile. Climb it and at a fork immediately ahead, take the right-hand lower path. By a fingerpost at the next fork, take the left-hand path, signposted Middle Walk, eventually passing beside a gate and keeping ahead to a road. Turn left and follow the road around a left bend to return to the start. ●

Malpas

Start	Malpas
Distance	9 miles (14.5km)
Approximate time	4½ hours
Parking	Malpas
Refreshments	Pubs and cafés at Malpas, pub near point **F**
Ordnance Survey maps	Explorer 257 (Crewe & Nantwich), Landranger 117 (Chester & Wrexham)

This lengthy but undemanding walk explores the attractive and gently undulating countryside of south-west Cheshire to the south and east of Malpas and close to both the Shropshire and Welsh borders. From many points there are fine views looking across to the hills of North Wales. About two-thirds of the way round, the route passes by the old and new St Chad's churches at Tushingham.

From its hilltop position Malpas looks across the borderlands to Wales, and the large mound next to the church is the site of a Norman castle that was built to guard the border. The 14th- to 15th-century sandstone church, unusually large and imposing for a village church, contains some interesting gargoyles and impressive monuments. Nearby are some black and white, half-timbered cottages and houses.

Start in the village centre at the junction of Church Street and High Street and walk up Church Street to the church. Turn left along a track called Parbutts Lane to a kissing-gate, go through and walk along the left edge of a field. At a crossways by a kissing-gate on the left, turn right, head gently downhill across the field and go through a kissing-gate onto a lane **A**. Keep ahead, follow the lane around a right bend and take the first lane on the left **B**. Follow this winding lane for just over a mile (1.6km) to a T-junction and turn left **C** along a narrow lane signposted to Lower Wych. Keep ahead through the hamlet, after which the lane ascends and continues to a T-junction.

Turn left, at a public bridleway sign turn right through a gate **D** and bear left across a field. After skirting the left edge of a pond, bear right and make for a gate in the far right corner. Go through, keep ahead across the next field, passing to the right of another pond, and continue to the left-hand corner where you turn left through a gate. Veer slightly right across a field, go through a gate in the corner into the next field and continue along an enclosed track. This may well be muddy. Go through a gate, keep ahead and the track bends left to another gate. Go through that one and keep ahead to go through one more onto a road.

Turn left, at a public bridleway sign turn right **E** through a gate and walk along the left edge of a field. Go through another gate, keep along the right edge of the next field and in the corner, go through a gate and cross a bridge over a disued railway. Go through another gate, continue along the right edge of the next three fields, going through two more gates, and in the corner of the last field, turn right through another gate and turn left along the left edge of the next field. Go through a gate by a black and white cottage, continue along an enclosed

track, going through two gates, and keep ahead to a road on joining a tarmac track **F**. Turn right – there is a pub just ahead – and at a public footpath sign to Sandstone Trail, turn left along a hedge-lined track to the A41.

Carefully cross this busy road, take the enclosed tarmac track ahead and where it ends, bear right through a kissing-gate and follow a track across a field towards a brick-built church. This is old St Chad's Church, built in 1689 on the site of an earlier timber-framed

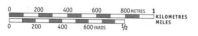

building. When a new church was built ½ mile (800m) away in 1863 to serve the parish of Tushingham, the old church was left standing in the fields on its own.

About 100 yds (91m) before reaching the church, turn left and head across the field to a stile. Climb it, keep ahead across the next field – following Marches Way not Sandstone Trail directions – and in the far corner, go through the right hand one of two kissing-gates. As you continue across the next field, the Victorian new church of St Chad's is seen over to the left. Climb a stile in the corner, turn left to cross the A41 again, turn right and take the first lane on the left, signposted to Bradley.

At a public footpath sign, turn right over a stile 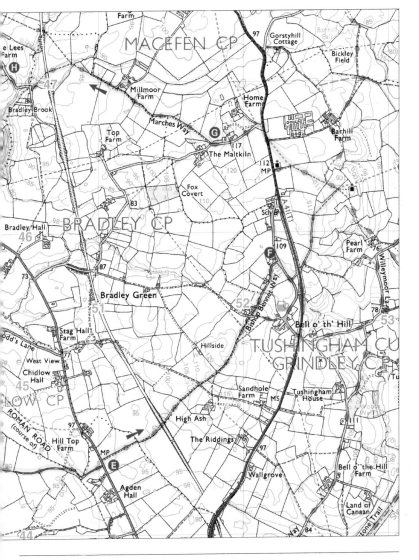 and walk along the right edge of a field to a gate. Go through, keep along the right edge of the next field, climb a stile and head gently downhill along the right edge of a field, passing to the left of a farm. Look out for where you turn right over a stile, turn left to continue along a left field edge and this time look out for where you turn left over a stile. Turn right, veer left away from the field edge to cross a footbridge and keep ahead to a stile.

After climbing it, head uphill across a field, bearing left to the top left-hand corner where you turn left through a gate and continue along a tree-lined embankment, part of a former railway track. Turn right and descend the embankment to go through a gate. Keep ahead along the edge of another embankment and descend to climb a stile onto a lane. Keep ahead uphill along this narrow lane, follow it around a right bend and at a public footpath sign, turn left through a kissing-gate **Ⓗ**. Walk diagonally across a field, later

bearing left along its left edge to go through a kissing-gate, and continue across the next field – there is a superb view ahead of Malpas – heading down by the right edge to a kissing-gate. Go through, turn right along a track and on entering a field, bear left along its left edge.

Cross a track, go through a kissing-gate and keep ahead, passing to the right of a pool and making for a kissing-gate. After going through it, keep ahead across the next field, go through another kissing-gate on the far side and continue along a tarmac path to a road. Turn left, follow the road to the right and turn left at a T-junction. At the next T-junction, turn right to return to the start. ●

Malpas

Mow Cop and Little Moreton Hall

Start	Mow Cop
Distance	8½ miles (13.6km) Shorter walk 5½ miles (8.8km)
Approximate time	4 hours (3 hours for short walk)
Parking	National Trust car park at Mow Cop
Refreshments	Pub at Mow Cop, tearoom at Little Moreton Hall
Ordnance Survey maps	Explorer 268 (Wilmslow, Macclesfield & Congleton), Landranger 118 (Stoke-on-Trent & Macclesfield)

Starting on a ridge, the route initially descends across fields and through woodland, with fine views over the Cheshire plain, to the Macclesfield Canal. It then continues across fields to Little Moreton Hall before returning to the canal. Then comes a steady climb through woodland and across open moorland to regain the ridge for the final stretch back to Mow Cop. The shorter version omits the extension to Little Moreton Hall.

The 'castle' at Mow Cop is a folly, a mock ruin built by a local landowner in 1754 to enhance the view. At a meeting on this rocky summit in 1807 the Primitive Methodist movement was born.

🖋 At a Gritstone Trail sign, take the path towards the left of the folly, at a fork continue along the left-hand path to a track and bear left to a road. Turn right and at a public footpath sign to Old Man of Mow, turn left along a track which bends left in front of houses and then turns right to pass to the left of the Old Man, a rock pinnacle created by quarrying. At a fingerpost just in front of a radio mast, **A** turn left – following South Cheshire Way signs – and head gently downhill, by a wire fence on the left, to a stile. Climb it, keep along the left edge of two fields, before climbing a stile into woodland, and continue downhill to a T-junction. Turn left to

climb a stile on the edge of the trees, turn right downhill along the right edge of a field and at a hedge corner, keep ahead across the field to a gate.

Go through, walk along a track, turn right at a T-junction, in the Ackers Crossing direction, and continue downhill along an enclosed track to the next T-junction. Turn left along a tarmac track, carefully cross a railway line and keep ahead to another T-junction. Turn right along New Road and cross a bridge over the Macclesfield Canal **B**.

For the short walk, turn sharp right, descend steps to the canal and turn left along the towpath.

For the extension to Little Moreton Hall, follow the road around right and left bends and at a public footpath sign, turn left over a stile. Head diagonally across a field, making for a stile on the far side, and after climbing it, keep in the same direction across the next field and climb another stile. Head gently uphill, bearing slightly left to climb a stile, continue across the next field and climb a stile onto a track **C**.

Turn right, climb a stile, turn right again and continue along the right edge of the next two fields. After climbing a stile into the third field, bear right, head diagonally across it and climb a stile in the far corner. Keep ahead to climb another stile, walk along the right edge of the next field, climb a stile and continue along a tarmac drive to Little Moreton Hall **D**.

This is one of the most photographed houses in England, its picturesque quality admired by producers of birthday cards and calendars. It was built in the late 15th to 16th centuries as the home of the Moreton family, local gentry, and has remained virtually unaltered since Elizabethan times.

Retrace your steps to the canal bridge **B** and turn left along the towpath to rejoin the shorter walk.

Little Moreton Hall

After passing under bridge 83, turn left up steps to a lane **E** and turn left again to cross the bridge. Keep ahead to cross a railway bridge, follow the lane around a left bend and where Oak Lane comes in from the left, turn right **F** along a tarmac track. At a public footpath sign opposite a farm, turn left onto a track – this may be muddy – that keeps by the left inside edge of woodland and bear left across a duckboard to a stile. Climb it, turn right along the right edge of a field and at a footpath post, turn right down steps and cross a series of three plank footbridges, plus a stile. After the last bridge, turn right onto an enclosed, wooded path which heads steadily uphill beside a brook – the path later widens into a track – to a stile.

Climb it, keep ahead and when you see a track heading off to the right

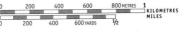

through trees, turn onto it and climb a stile. Keep ahead by the curving right edge of woodland, heading up to climb another stile, and continue, by a hedge on the right, to a fingerpost **G**. Turn right, walk along a low causeway – keeping parallel to the right edge of the field – climb a stile in a hedge and keep in the same direction across the next field. After going through a former hedgebank, continue gently uphill across rough, badly-drained, grassy moorland, eventually climbing a stile onto a tarmac track. The path is difficult to spot but for most of the time it follows a low causeway that is just about discernible.

After climbing the stile, keep ahead along the tarmac track up to a road and turn right. The road runs along a ridge and there are superb views both sides. At the drive to Roe Park Farm, bear right **H** – there is a Gritstone Trail post here – along a narrow, winding, undulating path through trees. Bear left on meeting another path, continue below an embankment on the left and look out for where a path turns left and heads steadily up the embankment between heather.

Keep by a wall on the left, passing to the right of a radio mast, to a T-junction and turn right along a track. Here you pick up the outward route and retrace your steps to the start. ●

Bulkeley Hill and Raw Head

Start	Higher Burwardsley, Candle Workshops, signposted from A41 and A49
Distance	6 miles (9.6km)
Approximate time	3 hours
Parking	Candle Workshops
Refreshments	Pub at Higher Burwardsley, café at the Candle Workshops
Ordnance Survey maps	Explorer 257 (Crewe & Nantwich), Landranger 117 (Chester & Wrexham)

Much of the route is along the well-wooded sandstone ridge that runs across Cheshire. After climbing Bulkeley Hill, you continue to Raw Head which, at 745 ft (227m), is the highest point on the ridge and, not surprisingly, a magnificent viewpoint. Indeed the whole walk provides a succession of similarly superb viewpoints from relatively modest heights and for relatively little effort as most of the climbing is steady rather than strenuous. There is, however, one steep descent soon after leaving Raw Head.

At the Candle Workshops – sometimes called Cheshire Workshops – there is a shop and café and you can watch how candles are made and see demonstrations of glass sculpture.

View from Raw Head

Begin by turning left out of the car park, at a fork take the right hand lane and at a crossroads, keep ahead along a lane signposted as a No Through Road. Head uphill, continue along the right hand lane at a fork and where it becomes a rough track, turn right over a stile Ⓐ to join the Sandstone Trail.

Walk along the left edge of a field, go through a kissing-gate and keep ahead along an enclosed path to go through another kissing-gate. Continue along a left field edge, climb a stile, keep along the left edge of the next field and in the corner, bear left to climb a stile. Descend steps, turn left along a

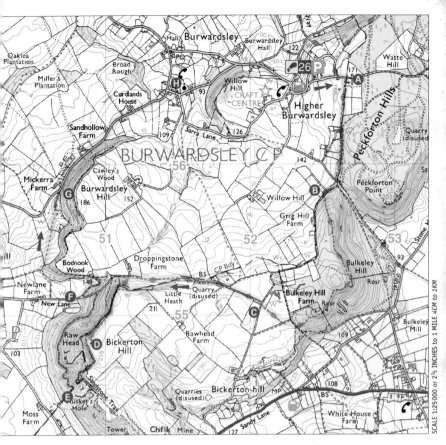

| 0 | 200 | 400 | 600 | 800 METRES | 1 |
| 0 | 200 | 400 | 600 YARDS | ½ | KILOMETRES / MILES |

SCALE 1:25 000 or 2½ INCHES to 1 MILE 4CM to 1KM

tarmac track and almost immediately turn right, at a Sandstone Trail sign, along a track by the right edge of Bulkeley Hill Wood. At the next Sandstone Trail waymark, turn left **B** and climb steps through the trees. Head quite steeply up to the top of Bulkeley Hill and as you continue along a wooded ridge, fine views open up on the left. Follow the curving ridge top first to the right and then to the left, pass through a fence gap and descend to a kissing-gate on the edge of the wood.

Go through, bear right diagonally across a field and go through a kissing-gate onto a track (Coppermines Lane) **C**. Continue along the track opposite and where it bears left, keep ahead along a tree-lined path. Look out for where a Sandstone Trail sign directs you to turn left through a kissing-gate and continue along a path which heads steadily uphill through more woodland, via steps in places. The path passes rocky outcrops and later keeps by a fence bordering a field on the left to reach the triangulation pillar on Raw Head, **D** the highest point on the Sandstone Trail, 745 ft (227m). Despite the modest height, the extensive views across Cheshire are magnificent.

At the summit, bear left to continue along the top of the wooded ridge and the path later bends right to descend a flight of steps. Keep ahead, follow the path around a left bend and at a waymarked post, turn right to leave the Sandstone Trail. At the next waymarked post, turn sharp right **E** and head steeply downhill through trees to a track at a U-bend. Bear right and the track winds across the face of the thickly-wooded hill to emerge onto a narrow tarmac track. Turn sharp left downhill and at a public footpath sign, turn sharp right along a track .

Just before the track curves left, turn left over a stile, walk across a field to a footpath post and continue past it to climb a stile into Bodnook Wood. At first keep along the top right inside edge of the wood, then continue through it and descend to climb a stile on the edge of the trees. Immediately turn right over another stile and head diagonally downhill across a field to a stile on the far side. Climb it, continue along the top right edge of the next field and climb a stile onto a road .

Keep ahead, take the first lane on the right (Church Road) and at a fork, take the left hand lane,  passing Burwardsley's small church, mainly 18th-century with a Victorian bell turret. The lane continues below the wooded slopes of Willow Hill to a T-junction. Turn right and at a fork, take the right hand lane through Higher Burwardsley, heading up to a junction. The pub is to the left but to return to the start, turn sharp right along Barracks Lane. ●

Raw Head

Shutlingsloe

Start	Trentabank car park, on minor road about 1½ miles (2.4km) east of Langley
Distance	6½ miles (10.4km)
Approximate time	3½ hours
Parking	Trentabank
Refreshments	Pub at Wildboarclough, pub at point **G**
Ordnance Survey maps	Explorer OL24 (The Peak District – White Peak area), Landranger 118 (Stoke-on-Trent & Macclesfield)

Shutlingsloe rises to a height of 1659 feet (506m) and its distinctive appearance earns for it the title of the 'Cheshire Matterhorn'. The climb to the summit – initially through the conifers of Macclesfield Forest and later over open moorland – is steady rather than steep and strenuous and is mostly on paved paths. After descending into Wildboarclough, the remainder of the route contours around the sides of the hill, involving quite a lot of 'ups and downs', before the final descent into the forest. Choose a fine and clear day as the views from these westerly fringes of the Peak District are immense.

Turn right, at a Forest Walks sign, not along the lane but along a parallel path through the trees, to a kissing-gate. Go through and turn right **A** onto a path which heads steadily uphill through the forest, keeping on the main path all the while and following regular footpath signs to Shutlingsloe.

At a crossways, turn right and continue uphill to a kissing-gate. Go through, keep ahead at the first fingerpost but at the next one, turn right, in the Shutlingsloe direction, onto a path which keeps along the right inside edge of the trees before bending right to another kissing-gate **B**. Go through and follow a paved path – there are steps in places – uphill across open moorland, later levelling out to reach a stile. Climb it, immediately turn right to

continue along a paved path, by a wall on the right, and after climbing a ladder stile, there follows the final, short, steep pull up to the triangulation pillar on the 1659-ft (506-m) summit **C**.

The views are tremendous, especially looking westwards across the Cheshire plain to Greater Manchester, Merseyside

Summit of Shutlingsloe

and – in clear conditions – the hills of North Wales. A yellow arrow on the triangulation pillar indicates the way down along a rocky path which bends right and winds steeply downhill, continuing across rough moorland to a fingerpost. Keep ahead to climb a stile, descend steps and continue gently downhill to another stile. Climb it, turn right alongside a wall on the left, follow the path around a left bend and continue down to a tarmac track.

Turn right, head downhill to a lane in the hamlet of Wildboarclough and turn right. Just beyond the Crag Inn, turn right **D** over a stone stile and follow a path which skirts the side of the hill, keeping parallel to the lane below and heading up between gorse bushes to a footpath post. Bear right across the grass to climb a stone stile and now the route continues more or less in a straight line across a series of fields and

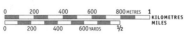

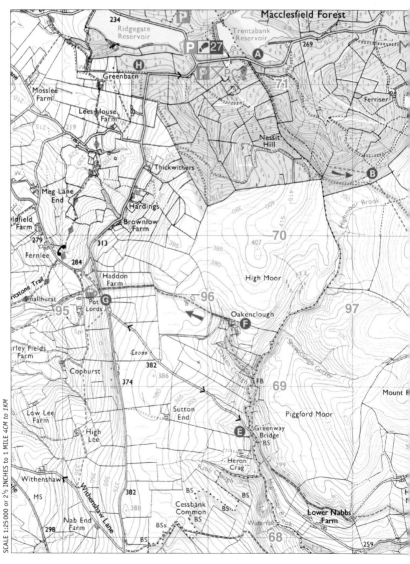

over a succession of stiles. Finally you head up to a waymarked gatepost and bear left along a track.

Immediately after climbing a stile, bear right onto a path by a wall on the right and climb a stone stile onto a tarmac track. Turn left and the track

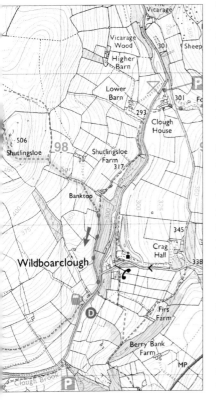

Shutlingsloe

gently descends to a lane. Bear right and just before the lane starts to ascend, turn right **E** over a stile, at a public footpath sign, and follow a path through the beautiful Oaken Clough, by a stream on the left. Climb a stile, cross the stream, continue through the valley and look out for a stile above you. Bear right steeply uphill to climb it, turn left by a fence on the right and bear right up to a stone stile. Climb it, turn left **F** along a tarmac track and where it bends left, go through a gate.

Head uphill along an enclosed path to a stile. Climb it, follow a path across open moorland, veering gradually right, and look out for where a waymark directs you to turn right between redundant gateposts. Turn left over a stile, head downhill along an enclosed path – you may have to share it with a stream – and at the bottom, climb a stile onto a road by the Hanging Gate Inn **G**.

Turn right and where the road bends sharply left, keep ahead along a lane which descends and re-enters the conifers of Macclesfield Forest. Follow the lane around a right bend, **H** continue downhill to a T-junction and turn right to return to the start. ●

Tegg's Nose and Macclesfield Forest

Tegg's Nose and Macclesfield Forest

Start	Tegg's Nose Country Park, signposted from Macclesfield town centre
Distance	8½ miles (13.7km) Shorter walk 7½ miles (12.1km)
Approximate time	4½ hours (4 hours for shorter version)
Parking	Tegg's Nose Country Park
Refreshments	None
Ordnance Survey maps	Explorer OL24 (Peak District – White Peak area), Landranger 118 (Stoke-on-Trent & Macclesfield)

After the initial descent from the country park, you continue through the conifers of Macclesfield Forest to the Forest Chapel. The remainder of the route is an undulating one – mostly across fields, rough pasture and moorland – and there is likely to be some muddy stretches. The last 1¼ miles (2km) is along the well-waymarked Gritstone Trail. The full walk includes a short additional stretch at the end to the viewpoint of Tegg's Nose. This is quite a strenuous walk with lots of climbs and descents, sometimes over rough ground, and it is not advisable to attempt it in bad weather, especially in misty conditions, unless experienced in walking in such conditions and able to navigate by using a compass.

Start by taking the paved downhill path, signposted Saddlers Way, go through a gate and continue down to a lane **Ⓐ**. Keep ahead downhill and after going round a sharp left bend in front of the entrance to Clough House, the lane becomes first an enclosed track and then an uphill, enclosed path.

The path bends right, heads downhill to ford a stream and continues uphill. At the top, turn left along another enclosed path and in front of a farm, turn right along a narrow lane. Follow it around a left bend and immediately turn right over a stile, **Ⓑ** at a public footpath sign, to enter Macclesfield

Forest. The present forest comprises a number of mainly conifer woods occupying the western slopes of the Peak District and overlooking the Cheshire plain, and is just a small part of what was, in the Middle Ages, a large, royal, hunting forest. Much of it would have been, as today, open moorland rather than thick woodland.

Take the path through the trees and at a junction, turn right, in the Forest Chapel direction. On emerging into a clearing by a ruined hut, bear left to a crossways, keep ahead through a gate and over a stile and head uphill – there are steps in places – to negotiate another stile and gate combination. Keep ahead up more steps, continue uphill through dense woodland and the path later flattens out to reach a stile on the edge of the forest. Climb it, bear right along an enclosed track which descends to a lane and turn left, **C** signposted No Through Road, to the Forest Chapel.

This plain and simple church was built in 1673 and reconstructed in 1831. It is one of a number of churches where a rushbearing ceremony is held to commemorate the annual renewal of the rushes, which originally covered most church floors. At a public footpath sign, turn left over a stone stile, walk along an enclosed path, climb two stiles in quick succession and walk downhill along the left edge of a field to another stile. Climb that one – a boardwalk enables you to cross a stream and boggy ground – head uphill along the left edge of a field, climb a stile and keep along the left edge of the next field, marked by a low hedgebank. Continue over the brow and descend to a stile.

Climb it, head downhill along the left edge of a field, climb another stile, cross a stream and keep ahead uphill again. Walk past a waymarked post and at the next one, turn left up to another post and bear right towards a farm. Climb a stone stile into the farmyard, turn right by the house and continue along a track to a road. Cross over, climb the stile opposite, walk across a field and go through a gate onto the main Macclesfield-Buxton road **D**.

Cross over, climb the stone stile opposite and walk across a field, making for a stone stile on the far side. After climbing it, head across the corner of the next field and climb a ladder stile onto a lane. Turn left downhill and where the lane bears right, bear left **E** along a track, at a public footpath sign, to a stile. Climb it, continue along the track, by woodland bordering Lamaload Reservoir on the right, follow it around a right bend, climb a stile and head uphill to a fingerpost.

The main track bears left here but

Approaching Tegg's Nose

keep ahead – still beside a wall and trees on the right – and at a fork, take the left hand track. Climb a stile, keep ahead and after climbing a stone stile, take a faint but discernible grassy path across a field to a footpath post and ladder stile. Climb the stile, continue along the path ahead through a conifer wood, climb another stile and head downhill by the left edge of the conifers. Climb a stile, keep ahead to a fingerpost, turn left over another stile and walk along an enclosed path which curves right to a tarmac track by the entrance to Lamaload Water Treatment Works **F**.

Turn left, head uphill, follow the

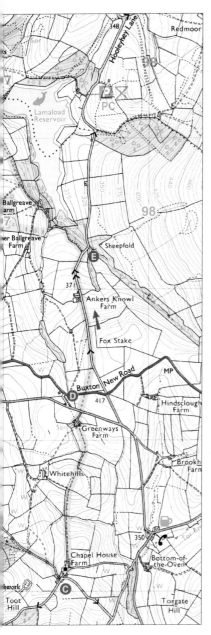

quick succession, continue uphill along the right edge of a field and turn right over a ladder stile.

Head diagonally across the next field, climb a stone stile to the right of a gate and turn right along an enclosed track. Just after the track bears left, turn right **H** over a stile and walk along the right edge of a field, here joining the Gritstone Trail for the rest of the walk. Climb a stile, head diagonally across the next field to climb a waymarked ladder stile and descend steeply to cross a stream. Continue up to a waymarked post which directs you to turn left and walk across the field to a stile. Head uphill along the right edge of a field and after climbing a stile, continue diagonally uphill across the next field to a stile in the corner.

Climb it onto the main Macclesfield-Buxton road again **J**. Turn left and when you see a public footpath sign, cross the road, go up steps and through a gate and keep along the right edge of a field. After climbing a stile, bear left gently uphill across a field, climb another stile and bear right across the corner of the next field to a ladder stile. Climb it, keep in the same direction across a succession of fields and over a series of stiles, finally climbing a stone stile in the bottom right hand corner of the last field onto a track. Turn left to a road **K** and turn right to the start.

If doing the additional walk to the Tegg's Nose viewpoint – worthwhile not just for the view but also because the area is a maze of old quarry workings – keep ahead past the car park entrance and bear left along a well-surfaced track. Go through a kissing-gate, keep ahead and after going through another gate, the path bends left and heads up, passing by former quarrying equipment, to the viewpoint **L**. *From here retrace your steps to the start.* ●

track around a left bend and continue along it for a mile (1.6km) as it winds above the Dean valley. Just after passing a house on the left, turn left **G** over a stone stile, at a public footpath sign, and walk uphill across a field. After passing through a wall gap, bear left across the corner of a field, climb a stone stile and head diagonally uphill across the next field. Climb two stiles in

Further Information

The National Trust

Anyone who likes visiting places of natural beauty and/or historic interest has cause to be grateful to the National Trust. Without it, many such places would probably have vanished by now.

It was in response to the pressures on the countryside posed by the relentless march of Victorian industrialisation that the trust was set up in 1895. Its founders, inspired by the common goals of protecting and conserving Britain's national heritage and widening public access to it, were Sir Robert Hunter, Octavia Hill and Canon Rawnsley: respectively a solicitor, a social reformer and a clergyman. The latter was particularly influential. As a canon of Carlisle Cathedral and vicar of Crosthwaite (near Keswick), he was concerned about threats to the Lake District and had already been active in protecting footpaths and promoting public access to open countryside. After the flooding of Thirlmere in 1879 to create a large reservoir, he became increasingly convinced that the only effective way to guarantee protection was outright ownership of land.

The purpose of the National Trust is to preserve areas of natural beauty and sites of historic interest by acquisition, holding them in trust for the nation and making them available for public access and enjoyment. Some of its properties have been acquired through purchase, but many have been donated. Nowadays it is not only one of the biggest landowners in the country, but also one of the most active conservation charities, protecting 581,113 acres (253,176 ha) of land, including 555 miles (892km) of coastline, and more than 300 historic properties in England, Wales and Northern Ireland. (There is a separate National Trust for Scotland, which was set up in 1931.)

Furthermore, once a piece of land has come under National Trust ownership, it is difficult for its status to be altered. As a result of parliamentary legislation in 1907, the Trust was given the right to declare its property inalienable, so ensuring that in any subsequent dispute it can appeal directly to parliament.

As it works towards its dual aims of conserving areas of attractive countryside and encouraging greater public access (not easy to reconcile in this age of mass tourism), the Trust provides an excellent service for walkers by creating new concessionary paths and waymarked trails, maintaining stiles and footbridges and combating the ever-increasing problem of footpath erosion.

For details of membership, contact the National Trust at the address on page 95.

The Ramblers' Association

No organisation works more actively to protect and extend the rights and interests of walkers in the countryside than the Ramblers' Association. Its aims are clear: to foster a greater knowledge, love and care of the countryside; to assist in the protection and enhancement of public rights of way and areas of natural beauty; to work for greater public access to the countryside; and to encourage more people to take up rambling as a healthy, recreational leisure activity.

It was founded in 1935 when, following the setting up of a National Council of Ramblers' Federations in 1931, a number of federations earlier formed in London, Manchester, the Midlands and elsewhere came together to create a more effective pressure group, to deal with such problems as the disappearance and obstruction of footpaths, the prevention of access to open mountain and moorland and increasing hostility from landowners. This was the era of the mass trespasses, when there were sometimes violent confrontations between ramblers and gamekeepers, especially on the moorlands of the Peak District.

Gawsworth Hall

Since then the Ramblers' Association has played an influential role in preserving and developing the national footpath network, supporting the creation of national parks and encouraging the designation and waymarking of long-distance routes.

Our freedom to walk in the countryside is precarious and requires constant vigilance. As well as the perennial problems of footpaths being illegally obstructed, disappearing through lack of use or extinguished by housing or road construction, new dangers can spring up at any time.

It is to meet such problems and dangers that the Ramblers' Association exists and represents the interests of all walkers. The address to write to for information on the Ramblers' Association and how to become a member is given on page 95.

Walkers and the Law

The average walker in a national park or other popular walking area, armed with the appropriate Ordnance Survey map, reinforced perhaps by a guidebook giving detailed walking instructions, is unlikely to run into legal difficulties, but it is useful to know something about the law

relating to public rights of way. The right to walk over certain parts of the countryside has developed over a long period, and how such rights came into being is a complex subject, too lengthy to be discussed here. The following comments are intended simply as a helpful guide, backed up by the Countryside Access Charter, a concise summary of walkers' rights and obligations drawn up by the Countryside Commission.

Basically there are two main kinds of public rights of way: footpaths (for walkers only) and bridleways (for walkers, riders on horseback and pedal cyclists). Footpaths and bridleways are shown by broken green lines on Ordnance Survey Pathfinder and Outdoor Leisure maps and broken red lines on Landranger maps. There is also a third category, called byways: chiefly broad tracks (green lanes) or farm roads, which walkers, riders and cyclists have to share, usually only occasionally, with motor vehicles. Many of these public paths have been in existence for hundreds of years and some even originated as prehistoric trackways and have been in constant use for well over 2000 years. Ways known as RUPPs (roads used as public paths) still appear on some maps. The legal definition of such

Countryside Access Charter

Your rights of way are:

- public footpaths – on foot only.
  Sometimes waymarked in yellow
- bridle-ways – on foot, horseback and
  pedal cycle. Sometimes waymarked
  in blue
- byways (usually old roads), most
  'roads used as public paths' and, of
  course, public roads – all traffic has
  the right of way

Use maps, signs and waymarks to check
rights of way. Ordnance Survey Explorer
and Landranger maps show most public
rights of way

On rights of way you can:

- take a pram, pushchair or wheelchair
  if practicable
- take a dog (on a lead or under close
  control)
- take a short route round an illegal
  obstruction or remove it sufficiently to
  get past

*You have a right to go for
recreation to:*

- public parks and open spaces – on
  foot
- most commons near older towns and
  cities – on foot and sometimes on
  horseback
- private land where the owner has a
  formal agreement with the local
  authority

*In addition you can use the following by
local or established custom or consent,
but ask for advice if you are unsure:*

- many areas of open country, such as
  moorland, fell and coastal areas,
  especially those in the care of the
  National Trust, and some commons
- some woods and forests, especially
  those owned by the Forestry
  Commission
- country parks and picnic sites
- most beaches
- canal towpaths
- some private paths and tracks
  Consent sometimes extends to horse-
  riding and cycling

For your information:

- county councils and London boroughs
  maintain and record rights of way,
  and register commons
- obstructions, dangerous animals,
  harassment and misleading signs on
  rights of way are illegal and you
  should report them to the county
  council
- paths across fields can be ploughed,
  but must normally be reinstated
  within two weeks
- landowners can require you to leave
  land to which you have no right of
  access
- motor vehicles are normally permitted
  only on roads, byways and some
  'roads used as public paths'

byways is ambiguous and they are
gradually being reclassified as footpaths,
bridleways or byways.

The term 'right of way' means exactly
what it says. It gives right of passage over
what, in the vast majority of cases, is
private land, and you are required to keep
to the line of the path and not stray to
either side. If you inadvertently wander
off the right of way – either because of
faulty map-reading or because the route is
not clearly indicated on the ground – you
are technically trespassing and the wisest
course is to ask the nearest available
person (farmer or fellow walker) to direct
you back to the correct route. There are
stories about unpleasant confrontations
between walkers and farmers at times, but

in general most farmers are co-operative
when responding to a genuine and polite
request for assistance in route-finding.

Obstructions can sometimes be a
problem and probably the most common
of these is where a path across a field has
been ploughed up. It is legal for a farmer
to plough up a path provided that he
restores it within two weeks, barring
exceptionally bad weather. This does not
always happen and here the walker is
presented with a dilemma: to follow the
line of the path, even if this inevitably
means treading on crops, or to walk
around the edge of the field. The latter
course of action often seems the best but
this means that you would be trespassing
and not keeping to the exact line of the

path. In the case of other obstructions which may block a path (illegal fences and locked gates etc), common sense has to be used in order to negotiate them by the easiest method – detour or removal. You should only ever remove as much as is necessary to get through, and if you can easily go round the obstruction without causing any damage, then you should do so. If you have any problems negotiating rights of way, you should report the matter to the rights of way department of the relevant council, which will take whatever action is required with the landowner concerned.

Apart from rights of way enshrined by law, there are a number of other paths available to walkers. Permissive or concessionary paths have been created where a landowner has given permission for the public to use a particular route across his land. The main problem with these is that, as they have been granted as a concession, there is no legal right to use them and therefore they can be extinguished at any time. In practice, many of these concessionary routes have been established on land owned either by large public bodies such as the Forestry Commission, or by a private one, such as the National Trust, and as these mainly encourage walkers to use their paths, they are unlikely to be closed unless a change of ownership occurs.

Walkers also have free access to country parks (except where requested to keep away from certain areas for ecological reasons, eg. wildlife protection, woodland regeneration, safeguarding of rare plants etc), canal towpaths and most beaches. By custom, though not by right, you are generally free to walk across the open and uncultivated higher land of mountain, moorland and fell, but this varies from area to area and from one season to another – grouse moors, for example, will be out of bounds during the breeding and shooting seasons and some open areas are used as Ministry of Defence firing ranges, for which reason access will be restricted. In some areas the situation has been clarified as a result of 'access agreements' made between the landowners and either the county council or the national park authority, which clearly define when and where you can walk over such open country.

Mow Cop

Further Information

Safety on the Hills

The hills, mountains and moorlands of Britain, though of modest height compared with those in many other countries, need to be treated with respect. Friendly and inviting in good weather, they can quickly be transformed into wet, misty, windswept and potentially dangerous areas of wilderness in bad weather. Even on an outwardly fine and settled summer day, conditions can rapidly deteriorate. In winter, of course, the weather can be even more erratic and the hours of daylight are much shorter.

It is advisable, therefore, always to take both warm and waterproof clothing, sufficient nourishing food, a hot drink, first-aid kit, torch and whistle. Wear suitable footwear, ie. strong walking boots or shoes that give a good grip over rocky terrain and on slippery slopes. Try to obtain a local weather forecast and bear it in mind before you start. Do not be afraid to abandon your proposed route and return to your starting point in the event of a sudden and unexpected deterioration in the weather. Do not go alone. Allow enough time to finish the walk well before nightfall.

Most of the walks described in this book do not venture into remote wilderness areas and will be safe to do, given due care and respect, at any time of year in all but the most unreasonable weather. Indeed, a crisp, fine winter day often provides perfect conditions for walking, with firm ground underfoot and a clarity that it is not possible to achieve in the other seasons of the year. A few walks in this book, however, are suitable only for reasonably fit and experienced hill walkers who are able to use a compass, and these routes should definitely not be tackled by anyone else during the winter months or in bad weather, especially high winds and mist. These are indicated in the general description that precedes each of the walks.

Useful Organisations

Council for the Protection of Rural England
128 Southwark Street, London SE1 0SW
Tel. 020 7981 2800

Barthomley